Isagoge: A Classical Primer on Logic

الرِسَــــالَة الأثيرية

ISAGOGE

A Classical Primer on Logic

Athīr al-Dīn al-Abharī

(d. 663/1265)

إيسَاغُوجِي رِسَالَةٌ فِي المَنْطِقِ

أثير الدين المفضّل بن عمر الأبهري

Translation and Explanatory Notes

Feryal Salem

Blue Mountain Press
Chicago

First Published in 2022 by Blue Mountain Press

Isagoge: A Classical Primer on Logic is © Copyright 2022 by Feryal Salem, and all rights are reserved. No part of this book may be reproduced in any form without prior permission of Feryal Salem.

Library of Congress Control Number: 2021925559

ISBN: 978-0-578-33127-0 (paper)

No part of this book may be reproduced in any form without prior permission of the publisher. All rights reserved.

Printed in the United States of America

First printing, First editon

1 2 3 4 5 6 7 8 9

Set in Brill 11/15 and Sakkal Kitab 14/21

Copyediting: Valerie Joy Turner

Layout design and Typesetting: Scholarlytype

Table of Contents

Translator's Preface

The *Isagoge* of Athīr al-Dīn al-Abharī (*al-Risālat al-Athīriyya*): A Classical Primer on Logic

What Is Logic and Why Study It?

The word "logic" is derived from the Greek root word *logos*, meaning "reason" or "word." In Arabic, logic is translated as *manṭiq*, derived from the root n-ṭ-q, which means "to speak." The field of logic presupposes that the foundation of speaking clearly and articulating one's claims persuasively requires an understanding of how to make sound arguments. In the context of Islamic studies, the study of logic is essential for a sophisticated understanding of theology (*kalām*) and methodology of jurisprudence (*uṣūl al-fiqh*). Many of the arguments for the existence of God, theodicy, and discussions regarding divine attributes would be unintelligible without a basic ability to think clearly. Similarly, the format of Islamic legal methodology relies heavily on the reasoning skills and methods established in the study of logic.[1]

The goal of logic is to analyze the way in which knowledge is introduced into our minds. How can we describe the type of knowledge that is based on self-evident or axiomatic information? How can axiomatic concepts (*taṣawwurāt*) be categorized into groups? How can we perceive objects as distinct entities? When arriving at knowledge through a process of reasoning, how do we use axiomatic concepts as building blocks to make connections that result in what we call syllogisms? What kinds of information do syllogisms lead to and what makes them valid or invalid? The study of logic involves all of these questions, the foundations of which al-Abharī covers in his *Isagoge*.

Thus, we use logic to analyze how we know what we think we know in order to avoid flawed reasoning that may lead to faulty or invalid conclusions. This is especially relevant to specialists of Islamic studies

1 Ibrahim Emiroğlu, "Mantık," in *Islam Ansiklopedisi*, 28:18–28.

because many materials in classical texts, especially texts of theology and *fiqh*, use logical reasoning to derive conclusions. Logic was considered both a tool through which to understand and analyze Islamic texts and an art form that disciplines the mind through balanced thinking. It is for this reason that many Islamic texts on logic have titles that include terms such as "balance" (*mīzān*), "art" (*fann*), and "measurement" (*miʿyār*). Examples of the phrases used in philosophical texts include *ʿilm al-mīzān* (the science of balance), *fann al-mīzān* (the art of balance), *lisān al-mīzān* (the language of balance), *mīzān al-ʿuqūl* (the balance of minds), *miʿyār al-ʿilm* (the measurement of knowledge), or *al-qiṣṭāṣ al-mustaqīm* (the just balance).[2] Indeed, it is also for this reason that the study of logic has been, historically, an integral element of the curriculum of Islamic educational networks throughout the premodern Muslim world.

Athīr al-Dīn al-Abharī's Life, Teachers, and Works

Al-Abharī was one of the earliest students of Fakhr al-Dīn al-Rāzī (d. 606/1210); he played a significant role in establishing al-Rāzī's model of argumentation, philosophy, and theology. Al-Abharī's most famed works, the *Risālat al-athīriyya* (known as the *Isagoge*) and *Hidāyat al-ḥikma*, established his renown and were used for generations in educational networks throughout the Muslim world, from the western Islamic lands to the Indian subcontinent.

There are a variety of references to the birthplace of Athīr al-Dīn al-Mufaḍḍal b. ʿUmar al-Samarqandī al-Abharī (d. 663/1265). It is said that al-Abharī began his studies in Mosul, then moved to Khurasan and Baghdad. In addition to being a student of al-Rāzī, he was a contemporary of Naṣīr al-Dīn al-Ṭūsī (d. 672/1274).

Many later commentaries were written on al-Abharī's *Isagoge*. Among the most well-known commentaries are the *Fawāʾid al-Fanariyya* written by Mulla Fanārī (d. 834/1451), the first Shaykh

2 This list is derived from Ibrahim Emiroğlu, "Mantık," in *Islam Ansiklopedisi*, 28:19.

al-Islām of the Ottoman Empire, and *al-Maṭlaʿ sharḥ al-Īsāghūjī* of the renowned Cairene scholar Zakariyyā Muḥammad al-Anṣārī (d. 926/1519). The *Isagoge* was versified by ʿAbd al-Raḥmān al-Akhḍarī (d. 983/1575) in his *Sullam al-munawraq fi-l-manṭiq*, which became a prevalent source in North African and Mālikī contexts.[3] Al-Abharī's *Isagoge* was first translated into Latin in 1625 by P. Thomas Novariensis. Edwin Calverly later published an English translation of the *Isagoge* in the Duncan Black Macdonald Memorial Volume published in 1933.[4]

Other works composed by al-Abharī include (1) *Tanzīl al-afkār fī taʿdīl al-asrār*, (2) *Kashf al-ḥaqāʾiq fī taʾkhīr al-daqāʾiq*, (3) *Risālat al-bākhira fī maqālāt al-ẓāhira*, (4) *Kitāb al-maṭāliʿ*, (5) *Kitāb bayān al-asrār*, (6) *Talkhīṣ al-ḥaqāʾiq*, (7) *Zubdat al-asrār*, (8) *Tahdhīb al-nukat*, (9) *Risāla fī fasād al-abḥāth allatī waḍaʿahā mubriz al-jadaliyyīn*, and (10) *Risāla mushtamila ʿalā thamānī ʿashara masʾalatin fī al-kalām*. In addition to these works, al-Abharī also wrote a number of books on astronomy and geometry. Most of al-Abharī's works have not yet been published and are only available in manuscript form in libraries.[5]

A Brief History of Logic

Aristotle's works known as the *Organon* were given much attention for their use as a "tool" or instrument for acquiring knowledge. The word *organon* means "tool" in Greek. The six books known in Aristotelian logic as the *Organon* are (1) *Categories*, (2) *On Interpretation*, (3) *Prior Analytics*, (4) *Posterior Analytics*, (5) *Topics*, and (6) *On Sophistical Refutations*. Later commentators in the Western tradition consider (7) *Rhetoric*, (8) *Poetics*, and (9) Porphyry's *Isagoge* to be part of the *Organon*.

While modern histories on the spread and evolution of ancient philosophy tend to center on modern-day Europe as the region in

3 Abdulkuddüs Bingöl, "Īsāgūcī," in *Islam Ansiklopedisi*, 22:488–489.

4 G. C. Anawati, "Abharī, Aṯīr-al-dīn," in *Encyclopædia Iranica*, I/2:216–217; E. Calverly, *D. B. Macdonald Memorial Volume* (Princeton, NJ, 1933), 75–85.

5 Abdulkuddüs Bingöl, "Ebheri, Esirüddin," in *Islam Ansiklopedisi*, 10:75–76.

which philosophy emerged and evolved, a far more comprehensive history of philosophy emerging from ancient Greece reveals that in fact regions east of modern-day Greece—places such as Asia Minor (modern-day Turkey), Jundishapur (near Baghdad), parts of the Syrian coast, and Alexandria adopted the ideas of Aristotle, Socrates, Plato, and Plotinus before they became prevalent in Europe. When Muslims settled in these regions and/or when individuals from these lands converted to Islam, the cultural practices and intellectual trends of these regions merged into the cosmopolitanism of Muslim lands that hosted a variety of faiths and schools of thought under the umbrella of Islamicate civilizations. Thus, what began as Greek philosophy under the pagan Greeks was studied by Greek-speaking Middle Eastern Christians who were later the mediums through which Muslim philosophers acquired these ideas.

As a result of this eastward spread, regions like Baghdad and Samarqand became new centers for the study of ancient philosophy. Here Muslim attitudes toward Greek philosophy were diverse and a variety of beliefs were tolerated and openly debated. Greek philosophical texts were first translated into Arabic by Arab Christians in Syria and Iraq who were trained in the Greek and Syriac used in biblical texts. The ʿAbbāsid rulers were great patrons of philosophers; under the caliph al-Ma'mūn a movement to translate philosophical texts into Arabic in a systematic fashion emerged in an academy known as the House of Wisdon (Bayt al-Ḥikma).

As philosophy became rooted in Arabic among Muslim thinkers, later Muslim philosophers did not simply preserve Greek philosophical texts in Arabic, rather they engaged with them and produced literature to substantively develop these ideas further. Ancient philosophy and Islamic thought merged to form a distinctly Islamic philosophical system that enriched the wisdom it inherited. Muslim philosophers debated, critiqued, and developed the ideas they encountered in an attempt to reconcile ancient philosophy with Islamic monotheism.

In the earliest phases of the development of philosophy in the Muslim world al-Kindī (d. 259/873) formed an essential bridge through which the works of Plotinus were transmitted into Arabic philosophical writings.[6] Almost one century later al-Fārābī (d. 339/950) expanded on the works of Aristotle; he organized the books of the *Organon* according to the following schema: (1) *al-Madkhal* (*Isagoge*), (2) *al-Maqūlāt* (*Categories*), (3) *al-'Ibāra* (*On Interpretation*), (4) *al-Qiyās* (*Prior Analytics*), (5) *al-Burhān* (*Posterior Analytics*), (6) *al-Jadal* (*Topics*), (7) *Kitāb al-ḥikma* (*On Sophistical Refutations*), (8) *al-Khiṭāba* (*Rhetoric*), (9) *al-Shi'r* (*Poetics*).

Ibn Sīnā (d. 428/1037; known in the West as Avicenna) was the unprecedented genius of the Greek philosophical tradition; his contribution permanently reshaped philosophy rooted in Platonic and Aristotelian thought into its new form. In the Islamic world, ancient philosophy became known through Ibn Sīnā and later Muslim theologians engaged, debated, and critiqued his works. They formulated answers to theological questions that had been both preserved and transformed by Ibn Sīnā's model.

As philosophy was developed by Muslims following the foundations set by al-Kindī, al-Farābī, and Ibn Sīnā, many of their ideas were challenged on a theological basis by Muslim thinkers who objected to some of their beliefs on creedal grounds. For instance, al-Ghazālī argued that three beliefs held by philosophers were antithetical to Islamic belief. Those he found objectionable were (1) the belief in the eternality of the universe, (2) the idea that God does not interfere in the particulars of life, and (3) the idea of the resurrection of the soul but not the body in the afterlife. Before al-Ghazālī's time, Muslim thinkers who objected to some of the creedal matters that philosophers delved into lacked the intellectual tools to challenge these ideas. Thus

---

6 This is despite the fact that al-Kindī had limited access to the complete works of Plotinus and throughout his work, he refers to Plotinus as Aristotle. See also Peter Adamson, *Philosophy in the Islamic World: A History of Philosophy Without Any Gaps* (Oxford: Oxford University Press, 2016).

many of them objected either through polemical exchanges or through disengagement. Al-Ghazālī saw that this approach did not adequately challenge what he deemed to be the problematic creedal elements of Islamic philosophy and that rather than polemics or avoidance, Muslim thinkers needed to find ways to engage philosophy using the same form of rational intellectual tools used by philosophers.

Rather than closing the door of reason as some contemporary scholars contended, al-Ghazālī in fact opened the doors for an engagement of philosophy by mainstream Sunnī theologians. This alternative narrative, that is, the idea that the door of reason did not close, is now becoming more prevalent in the Western academy through works that demonstrate that al-Ghazālī did not contradict philosophy altogether in his famous work *Incoherence of the Philosophers* (*Tahāfut al-falāsifa*), rather he used the rational methodology of engagement set by philosophers to demonstrate specific inconsistencies in some of their conclusions.[7] This effort was later taken up by the Ashʿarī Shāfiʿī scholar Fakhr al-Dīn al-Rāzī who completed the path opened by al-Ghazālī by rewriting theological texts in a way that incorporates the theologically relevant philosophical questions, such as the nature of existence and the physical world, into these discussions. Al-Rāzī used philosophy, which he refers to as *ḥikma* and which he includes in the texts of theology (*kalām*) to further develop philosophical discussions and challenge many of the beliefs of earlier philosophers, beliefs that he and other Muslims scholars regarded as both rationally inconsistent and creedally flawed.

This new school of theology based on al-Rāzī's model of engaging philosophical problems through similar rational methods included in philosophical texts became known as the post-classical or late (*muta'khkhirūn*) school of Ashʿarī theology. This school stood in contrast to the model of Ashʿarī theology prior to al-Ghazālī known as the classical school of Ashʿarism (*mutaqaddimūn*). Al-Abharī adopted

---

7 See also Frank Griffel, *The Formation of Post-Classical Philosophy in Islam* (Oxford: Oxford University Press, 2021).

the school of philosophical theology propagated by his teacher Fakhr al-Dīn al-Rāzī. His works on logic and philosophy follow al-Rāzī's structure and rationale that Sunnī theologians must be able to engage philosophers and their methodologies to effectively respond to the challenges they were deemed to pose to the mainstream creed.

Fakhr al-Dīn al-Rāzī and the Ottoman Intellectual Tradition

As mentioned, al-Rāzī built on al-Ghazālī's foundations by restructuring Ashʿarī theology to substantively engage and incorporate the major questions examined by philosophers. He refrained from polemical discourse and utilized a level of rigor in rational debate that placed Ashʿarī theology on an equal intellectual footing with philosophers in Ibn Sīnā's tradition. As a result, we can say that later Sunnī theology and philosophy were transformed when Ashʿarī theology was philosophized and Ibn Sīnā's philosophy was significantly reshaped under the framework of mainstream theological discourse.

Al-Rāzī's school of thought became prevalent and influenced various centers of learning throughout Ilkhānid- and Tīmūrid-era Iran and Transoxiana, before eventually becoming the foundation on which the Ottoman Islamic intellectual tradition of theology, philosophy, and Islamic law developed. Patronage of Islamic educational institutions and thinkers during the Ottoman era led to the continued flourishing of Ashʿarī and Māturīdī philosophical theology that many Ottoman theologians adhered to. In fact, we see a movement among theologians of this era to bring together the post-classical Ashʿarī and later Māturīdī schools.

The expanse of Ottoman lands and the length of Ottoman dominance as a world power ensured that their endowed scholastic networks, which excelled in the rational sciences (*ʿaqliyyāt*), cultivated the continued development of Islamic philosophy, logic, and theology (*kalām*) as foundational elements in Islamic education. In the Ottoman era, the establishment of al-Rāzī's model of rational discourse and philosophy of debate (*al-baḥth wa-l-munāẓara*) led to a new level of lively dialogue and exchange between Sunnī and Shīʿī thinkers based in the Ottoman and Ṣafavid scholastic networks. As a result, a discourse with a more reconciliatory tone between Ottoman Sunnī and Ṣafavid Shīʿī theologians emerged. Over time, substantial overlap and commonalities on matters related to philosophy and metaphysics led to discussion and debate between followers of these two streams of thought who engaged in rational discourse rather than polemics.

Examples of these intellectual engagements can be seen in the many commentaries on the Shīʿī scholar Naṣīr al-Dīn al-Ṭūsī's *Tajrīd al-ʿaqāʾid* by prominent Sunnī scholars such as Shams al-Dīn Maḥmūd b. ʿAbd al-Raḥmān al-Iṣfahānī (d. 749/1349) and al-Sharīf al-Jurjānī (d. 816/1413) whose works were later incorporated into the Ottoman educational system and elaborated on through the many commentaries on these commentaries. Sunnī commentaries on al-Ṭūsī's discussion of metaphysics and philosophy became a bridge of constructive dialogue between Sunnī and Shīʿī thinkers during the Ottoman era while al-Iṣfahānī's debate with al-Ṭūsī in his *Tasdīd al-qawāʿid fī sharḥ tajrīd al-ʿaqāʾid* on religious and political leadership (*imāma*) became a foundational section of the text studied in the Ottoman *madrasa* curriculum and shaped a distinctive Sunnī perspective on this topic.

Meanwhile, a major criticism of al-Rāzī's Islamic philosophical theology arose among a segment of the Maghribi school of Ashʿarī thelogians that included al-Tilimsānī and al-Sanūsī, who were highly critical of his incorporation of philosophy into books of theology. Sharaf al-Dīn al-Tilimsānī (d. 658/1259) was known for his sharp criticism of al-Rāzī in his commentary on al-Rāzī's *Maʿālim fī uṣūl al-dīn*; another Maghribi theologian, Muḥammad b. Yūsuf al-Sanūsī (d. 890/1495), was known to have forbidden beginners from reading the texts of al-Bayḍāwī (d. 685/1286), who followed the precedent set by al-Rāzī.

While the Maghribi school maintained al-Juwaynī's model of theology by preserving the school of the *mutaqaddimīn* (early Ashʿarī theologians), they were less influential than other learning centers because after the fall of al-Andalus, Islamic scholastic institutions in this geographic region lost many of their patrons. At the same time, there was a shift in the geographic center of Muslim intellectual developments from the prosperous economic centers of Nishapur, Samarqand, Bukhara, and Baghdad to the newly formed Ottoman Empire. After 600 years of power and the migration of Sunnī scholars to its lands from the ninth/fifteenth century onward, scholars based in Ottoman lands became prominent.

Thus, the various theologians (among them al-Bayḍāwī, ʿAḍud al-Dīn al-Ījī (d. 756/1355), al-Taftazānī, al-Sharīf al-Jurjānī, Sirāj al-Dīn Urmawī (d. 682/1283), Ṭaşköprüzāde (d. 968/1561), Ismail Gelenbevi (d. 1205/1791)) that built on al-Rāzī's thinking lay the foundation for the post-classical school of Ashʿarī theology. This school ensured that Muslim engagement with philosophy continued from the eighth/fourteenth century through the twelfth/eighteenth century.

Porphyry and His *Isagoge*

Porphyry (234–305 CE), known as Furfuryus in Arabic sources, was born to a Phoenician family in the city of Tyre (later known as Ṣūr, in modern-day southern Lebanon). His name was Malchus, which means "king" in Semitic languages. It is said that he was given the name Porphyrius when he was in Athens; the word Porphyrius means "one who wears purple," and may have been an allusion to the purple color worn by royalty. Other accounts state that he was given the name Basilieus, which is a Latinized version of his name that also means "king," and that the name Porphyrius refers to his connection to Tyre, which is known as the city of purple.[8]

Porphyry traveled to Athens to study with Longinus (213–273 CE) and then later to Rome, where he became a foremost student of Plotinus (204 or 205–270 CE). History later recognized Porphyry for his extensive works recording the philosophy of his teacher Plotinus in the *Enneads*.

8 See Jonathan Barnes, "Porphyry: Introduction" (Oxford: Oxford University Press, 2003), ix–x, for the latter claim.

Nineteenth-century historians considered Plotinus the founder of what they categorized as "Neoplatonism," a philosophical movement that restored Plato's teachings, particularly his emphasis on the reality of forms in the metaphysical realm, in response to the Hellenic schools of Epicureanism and Stoicism, which evolved after Aristotle, whose focus on the corporeal was criticized for being superficial.

In addition to recording the philosophy of Plotinus, Poryphyry authored a number of texts, some of which are no longer extant, though others remain (in part), such as the *Life of Plotinus,* the *Life of Pythagoras,* a *Letter to Marcella,* and *On Abstinence from Eating Food from Animals.*[9] One of the more well-known of these works was his *Isagoge*, a short treatise introducing Aristotle's six books known as the *Organon*. Some maintain that the *Isagoge* was just an introduction to Aristotle's *Categories.* Others argue that it is more likely that this work was designed to introduce beginners to the works of Aristotle, whose first work is the *Categories*.

Is al-Abharī's *Isagoge* a Version of Porphyry's *Isagoge*?

In the millennium between Porphyry's *Isagoge* and al-Abharī's *Isagoge* the genre of the *madkhal* (introduction, or *isagoge*) to logic evolved into a new form in its Islamic context. After Byzantium's conversion to Christianity in the fourth century, and because of the skepticism of many medieval Christian leaders, the study of philosophy was suppressed in ways that it had not been before. The works of Greek philosophers such as Aristotle were not limited to Byzantine lands, but also took root in the East. From the time of Alexander the Great who sought to spread Hellenic education through its texts, these works spread through the gates of Babylon and the Central Asian regions of the Bactrians.

Simply put, al-Abharī's *Isagoge* is not a translation of Porphyry's *Isagoge*. Al-Abharī inherited an intellectual lineage of philosophical

9 *Stanford Encyclopedia of Philosophy*: https://plato.stanford.edu/entries/porphyry/.

scholarship that engaged with and transformed Greek philosophy into Islamic philosophical theology, as discussed above. Although the *Isagoge* of Porphyry and that of al-Abharī share a title, by al-Abharī's time, Muslim philosophical theologians had significantly redefined words and concepts inherited from ancient philosophy and located them in their own contexts.

Thus, the similarity in title is incidental and does not indicate that one is a translation of the other. A preliminary examination of the contents of these two works makes this amply clear. Porphyry's *Isagoge* is entirely dedicated to outlining the five predicables (*quinque voces*); that is, the ways in which things can be classified. Porphyry lists these five predicables as species, difference, genus, property, and accident. By contrast, al-Abharī begins his *Isagoge* with a discussion of how we give meaning to objects, in fact he spends relatively little time on the predicables; his treatise focuses on how to form propositions and make sound arguments. Thus, the common error of assuming that the Arabic *Isagoge* authored by al-Abharī is the same as the *Isagoge* of Porphyry is easily clarified by a comparison of the contents of each. In his *Isagoge*, al-Abharī follows Ibn Sīnā's structure of outlining logic by dividing sections into concepts (*taṣawwurāt*) and assents (*taṣdīqāt*). This is a divergence from the Aristotelian organization of logic and demonstrates that al-Abharī's thought evolved from the time of Porphyry's work. A more detailed discussion of concepts and assents follows.

❋

مَتْنُ الرِسَـــالَةُ

The Text of the Primer

The Logic of Athīr al-Dīn al-Abharī

[1] The shaykh, erudite *imām*, best of the post-classical [scholars], model for the rooted philosophers, Athīr al-Dīn al-Abharī, may God make his resting place pleasant and make paradise his final abode, said: "We thank God the exalted for granting success, ask Him for guidance on His path, and we send prayers upon Muḥammad and the entirety of his kin."

[2] To proceed, this is a treatise in logic. We have conveyed in it what must be understood in order to begin studying any part of the sciences while depending on God, as He is the most generous source of goodness and abundance.

المَنْطِقِ لأَثِيرُ الدِّينِ المُفَضَّلُ بنِ عُمَر الْأَبْـهَرِيُّ

[١] قالَ الشَّيْخ الْإِمَامُ العلَّامَةُ أَفْضَلُ المُتَأَخِّرِينَ، قُدْوَةُ الحُكَمَاءِ الرَّاسِخِين أَثِيرُ الدِّينِ الْأَبْـهَرِيُّ، طَيَّبَ الله ثَرَاهُ، وَجَعَلَ الجَنَّةَ مَثْوَاهُ: نَحْمَدُ اللهَ تَعَالَى عَلَى تَوْفِيقِهِ، وَنَسْأَلُهُ هِدَايَةَ طَرِيقِهِ، وَنُصَلِّي عَلَى مُحَمَّدٍ وَعِتْرَتِهِ أَجْمَعِينَ.

[٢] أَمَّا بَعْدُ: فَهذِهِ رِسَالَةٌ فِي المَنْطِقِ، أَوْرَدْنَا فِيهَا مَا يَجِبُ اسْتِحْضَارُهَا لِمَنْ يَبْتَدِئُ فِي شَيْءٍ مِنَ الْعُلُومِ مُسْتَعِينًا بِاللهِ إِنَّهُ مُفِيضُ الْخَيْرِ وَالجودِ.

Isagoge

[3] Utterances that signify [meanings] by designating meaning to each articulated sound (*bi-l-waḍ'i*) can denote these meanings for which they [the utterances] have been posited, [either] in their entirety through a **full correlation** (*bi-l-muṭābaqa*); or [they can do so] in part through **inclusion** (*bi-l-taḍammun*), if [the meaning that an utterance refers to] is part [of this expression]; or [an utterance can designate a meaning through] what is associated (*yulāzimuhu*) with it in the mind. For example, [the word] "human" refers to a rational animal through full correlation, [and "human" refers] to one of the two categories [i.e., animal or rational being] through inclusion, and ["human" refers to one who is] inclined toward learning and the art of writing through **association** (*bi-l-iltizām*).

[4] **Expressions** are either **singular** (*mufrad*), such as the word "human" (*insān*), which does not convey a partial meaning if it were divided into two parts [such as *in* and *sān*]. Or they [expressions] can be compound (*mu'allaf*), such as [the expression] "rock thrower."

[5] A singular expression can be either **universal** (*kullī*), which is [an expression] that does not impede the conception of its meaning being shared among many, like the term "human." Or it can be a **particular** (*juz'ī*) [expression], which means it is an expression that prevents the conception of its meaning [being shared by many], like [for instance], "Zayd."

إيساغُوجِي

[٣] اللَّفْظُ الدَّالُّ بالوضْعِ، يَدُلُّ عَلَى تَمامِ مَا وُضِعَ لَهُ **بِالْمُطابَقَةِ**، وَعَلَى جُزْئِهِ **بِالتَّضَمُّنِ** إِنْ كَانَ لَهُ جُزْءٌ، وَعَلَى مَا يُلازِمُهُ فِي الذِّهْنِ **بِالإِلْتِزامِ**. كَالْإِنْسَانِ فَإِنَّهُ يَدُلُّ عَلَى الحيَوَانِ النَّاطِقِ بِالمُطَابَقَةِ، وَعَلَى أَحَدِهِمَا بِالتَّضَمُّنِ، وَعَلَى قابِلِ الْعِلْمِ وَصَنْعَةِ الْكِتَابَةِ بِالإِلْتِزَامِ.

[٤] **ثُمَّ اللَّفْظُ**: إِمَا **مُفْرَدٌ**: وَهُوَ الَّذِي لاَ يُرَادُ بِالجُزْءِ مِنْهُ دَلاَلَةٌ عَلَى جُزْءِ مَعْنَاهُ، كَالإِنْسَانِ. وَإِمَّا **مُؤَلَّفٌ**: وَهُوَ الَّذِي لاَ يَكُونُ كَذَلِكَ، كَرامِي الْحِجَارَةِ.

[٥] **وَالمُفْرَدُ**: إِمَّا **كُلِّيٌّ**: وَهُوَ الَّذِي لاَ يَمْنَعُ نَفْسُ تَصَوُّرِ مَفْهُومِهِ عَنْ وُقوعِ الشَّرِكَةِ بَيْنَ كَثِيرِينَ، كالإنسان. وَإِمَّا **جُزْئِيٌّ**: وَهُوَ الَّذِي يَمْنَعُ نَفْسُ تَصَوُّرِ مَفْهُومِهِ عَنْ ذَلِكَ، كَزَيْدٍ.

[6] Furthermore, a **universal** [expression] is either **essential** (*dhātī*), which means it constitutes the essential nature of each of [the] particulars [included in this universal term], such as [the word] "animal" in relation to "human" and "horse." Or [a universal expression] is **accidental** (*ʿaraḍī*), which means it contradicts this [principle mentioned above], such as laughing in relation to humans.

[7] The **essential** can be used as an answer to what something is in terms of a [broadly] shared identity, such as the term animal in relation to humans and horses. And this is [called] a **genus** (*jins*). [A genus] is described as a universal [property] that can be said of a variety of entities that differ in their true natures, [in] answer to [the question] of what it is.

[8] Alternatively, a [term] with both shared and specialized [properties] can be said to be an answer to the question, "what is it." For example, [one might use the word] "human" in reference to both Zayd and ʿAmr. This is [called] the **species** (*nawʿ*). It is described as a universal [term] that can be applied to numerous entities that do not differ in their true nature, [in] answer to [the question] of what it is.

[9] Or it could be that [one is not] responding [to the question] "what is it," but is instead responding to [the question] "what thing is it, in its essence?" This is what distinguishes it from other things it shares a genus with, such as [the quality of being] "rational," in regard to humans. This is called **differentia** (*faṣl*). It is described as a universal [property] that refers to an entity [in] answer to [the question] of "what is it in essence."

[٦] **وَالْكُلِّيُّ**: إِمَّا **ذَاتِيٌّ**: وَهُوَ الَّذِي يَدْخُلُ فِي حَقِيقَةِ جُزْئِيَّاتِهِ، كَالحَيَوَانِ بِالنِّسْبَةِ إِلَى الإِنْسَانِ وَالْفَرَسِ. وَإِمَّا **عرَضِيٌّ**: وَهُوَ الَّذِي يُخَالِفُهُ، كَالضَّاحِكِ بِالنِّسْبَةِ إِلَى الإِنْسَانِ.

[٧] **وَالذَّاتِيُّ**: إِمَا مَقُولٌ فِي جَوَابِ مَا هُوَ بِحَسَبِ الشَّرِكَةِ المَحْضَةِ، كَالحَيَوَانِ بِالنِّسْبَةِ إِلَى الإِنْسَانِ وَالْفَرَسِ، وَهُوَ **الجِنْسُ**؛ وَيُرْسَمُ بِأَنَّهُ كُلِّيٌّ مَقُولٌ عَلَى كَثِيرِينَ مُخْتَلِفِينَ بِالحَقَائِقِ فِي جَوَابِ مَا هُوَ.

[٨] وَإِمَّا مَقُولٌ فِي جَوَابِ مَا هُوَ بِحَسَبِ الشَّرِكَةِ وَالخُصُوصِيَّةِ مَعاً، كَالإِنْسَانِ بِالنِّسْبَةِ إِلَى زَيْدٍ وَعَمْرٍو، وَهُوَ **النَّوْعُ** ؛ وَيُرْسَمُ بِأَنَّهُ كُلِّيٌّ مَقُولٌ عَلَى كَثِيرِينَ مُخْتَلِفِينَ بِالْعَدَدِ دُونَ الحَقِيقَةِ فِي جَوَابِ مَا هُوَ.

[٩] وَإِمَّا غَيْرُ مَقُولٍ فِي جَوَابِ مَا هُوَ، بَلْ مَقُولٌ فِي جَوَابِ أَيُّ شَيْءٍ هُوَ فِي ذَاتِهِ، وَهُوَ الَّذِي يُمَيِّزُ الشَّيْءَ عمَّا يُشَارِكُهُ فِي الجِنْسِ، كَالنَّاطِقِ بِالنِّسْبَةِ إِلَى الإِنْسَانِ، وَهُوَ **الْفَصْلُ**؛ وَيُرْسَمُ بِأَنَّهُ كُلِّيٌّ يُقَالُ عَلَى الشَّيْءِ فِي جَوَابِ أَيُّ شَيْءٍ هُوَ فِي ذَاتِهِ.

[10] As for accidental [universals], their separation from the quiddity (*māhiya*) [of an entity] is inhibited and this is an **attached accident** (*'araḍ lāzim*), or their separation is not inhibited and this is a **detached accident** (*'araḍ al-mufāriq*). Each of these two [types of accidents] is specific to one true nature and this is the **property** (*khāṣṣa*). For example, [this could be] the capacity (*quwwa*) and act (*fi'l*) of laughing in relation to a human. It [laughter] is described as a universal that can be attributed to those with a single true nature [i.e., humans] as an accidental trait.

[11] Or it [the accidental universal] can be attributed to more than one true nature [e.g., not exclusively to humans] and is therefore a **general accident** (*'araḍ 'āmm*). This is like breathing in [terms of] capacity (*quwwa*) and action (*fi'l*) for humans and [for] others from [among] the animals. This [accidental universal] is described as a universal that can be applied to a variety of true natures (*ḥaqā'iq*) as an accidental trait.

[١٠] وَأَمَّا **الْعَرَضِيُّ**: فَإِمَّا أَنْ يَمْتَنِعَ انْفِكَاكُهُ عَنِ المَاهِيَّةِ وَهُوَ **الْعَرَضُ اللَّازِمُ**، أَوْ لا يَمْتَنِعَ وَهُوَ **الْعَرَضُ المُفَارِقُ**. وَكُلٌّ وَاحِدٍ مِنْهُمَا إِمَّا أَنْ يَخْتَصَّ بِحَقِيقَةٍ وَاحِدَةٍ، وَهِيَ الخَاصَّةُ، كَالضَّاحِكِ بِالْقُوَّةِ و بِالْفِعْلِ، بِالنِّسبَةِ إِلَى الإِنْسَانِ. وتُرْسَمُ بِأَنَّهَا كُلِّيَّةٌ تُقَالُ عَلَى مَا تَحْتَ حَقِيقَةٍ وَاحِدَةٍ فَقَطْ قَوْلاً عَرَضِيًّا.

[١١] وَإِمَّا أَنْ يَعُمَّ حَقَائِقَ فَوْقَ وَاحِدَةٍ، وَهُوَ **الْعَرَضُ الْعَامُّ**، كَالْمُتَنَفِّسِ بِالْقُوَّةِ وَبالْفِعْلِ لِلإِنْسَانِ وَغَيْرِهِ مِنَ الحَيَوانَاتِ .وَيُرسَمُ بِأَنَّهُ كُلِّيٌّ يُقَالُ عَلَى مَا تَحْتَ حَقَائِقَ مُخْتَلِفَةٍ قَوْلاً عَرَضِيّاً.

Expository Statement

[12] **Definition** (*ḥadd*): A statement that signifies the quiddity (*māhiya*) of a thing. It is composed of the close genus (*jins*) and close differentia (*faṣl,*) such as "rational animal" to [define] a human. This is also a **complete definition** (*ḥadd al-tāmm*).

[13] **Incomplete Definition** (*al-ḥadd al-nāqiṣ*): It is composed of a distant genus of a thing and a close differentia, such as "rational body" in reference to a human.

[14] **Complete Description** (*al-rasm al-tāmm*): It is composed of a close genus and a specific inseparable property (*khawāssihi al-lāzima*) such as a "laughing animal" to define a human.

[15] **Incomplete Description** (*al-rasm al-nāqiṣ*): It is composed of accidents whose combinations are specific to one true nature. For example, describing a human by saying that he walks on two feet, [he has] wide nails, a hairless body, [he] stands upright, and laughs by nature.

الْقَوْلُ الشَّارِحُ

[١٢] **الحَدُّ**: قَوْلٌ دَالٌّ عَلَى مَاهِيَّةِ الشَّيْءِ، وَ هُوَ الَّذِي يَتَرَكَّبُ مِنْ جِنْسِ الشَّيْءِ وَفَصْلِهِ الْقَرِيبَيْنِ، كَالحَيَوانِ النَّاطِقِ بِالنِّسْبةِ إِلَى الْإِنْسَانِ. وَهْوَ **الحَدُّ التَّامُّ**.

[١٣] **وَالحَدُّ النَّاقِصُ** : وَهُوَ الَّذِي يَتَرَكَّبُ مِنْ جِنْسِ الشَّيْءِ الْبَعِيدِ وَفَصْلِهِ الْقَرِيبِ، كَالجِسْمِ النَّاطِقِ بِالنِّسْبَةِ إِلَى الْإِنْسَانِ.

[١٤] **وَالرَّسْمُ التَّامُّ**: وَهْوَ الَّذِي يَتَرَكَّبُ مِنْ جِنْسِ الشَّيْءِ الْقَرِيبِ وَخَوَاصِّهِ اللَّازِمَةِ، كَالحَيَوانِ الضَّاحِكِ فِي تَعْرِيْفِ الْإِنْسَانِ.

[١٥] **وَالرَّسْمُ النَّاقِصُ**: وَهُوَ الَّذِي يَتَرَكَّبُ مِنْ عَرَضِيَّاتٍ تَخْتَصُّ جُمْلَتُهَا بِحَقِيقَةٍ وَاحِدَةٍ، كَقَوْلِنَا فِي تَعْرِيفِ الْإِنْسَانِ: إِنَّهُ مَاشٍ عَلَى قَدَمَيْهِ، عَرِيضُ الْأَظْفَارِ، بَادِي الْبَشَرَةِ، مُسْتَقِيمُ الْقَامَةِ، ضَحَّاكٌ بِالطَّبْعِ.

Propositions

[16] A proposition (*qaḍiyya*) is a statement about which it is valid to say to its claimant that he is truthful or untruthful [i.e., in his statement]. Additionally, it is either a categorical proposition (*ḥamliyya*), as in the phrase: "Zayd is a writer," or it is a conjunctive conditional proposition (*sharṭiyyatun muṭṭaṣila*), as in the statement: "If the sun has risen, it is daytime." Or it is a disjunctive conditional proposition (*sharṭiyyatun munfaṣila*), as in the statement: "Numbers are either even or odd." The first part of the categorical proposition (*ḥamliyya*) is known as the subject term (*mawḍūʿ*) and the second [part] is the predicate term (*maḥmūl*). The first part of the conditional [proposition] is termed the antecedent (*muqaddam*) and the second part is the consequent (*tālī*).

[17] A categorical proposition is either affirmative (*mūjiba*) as in our statement, "Zayd is a writer," or it is negative (*sāliba*), as in our statement, "Zayd is not a writer." Additionally, each of these is either **singular** (*makhṣūṣa*) as we mentioned or a **quantified universal proposition** (*kulliyya musawwara*), as in our statement, "every human is a writer" and "no human is a writer." Or [each of these propositions is] a **quantified particular proposition** (*juz'iyya musawwara*), as in our statement, "some humans are writers" and "some humans are not writers." Or it can be unlike these, in which case it is referred to as indefinite (*muhmala*), as in our statement, "the human is a writer" and "the human is not a writer."

الْقَضَايَا

[١٦] الْقَضِيَّةُ: قَوْلٌ يَصِحُّ أَنْ يُقَالَ لِقَائِلِهِ: إِنَّهُ صَادِقٌ فِيهِ أَوْ كَاذِبٌ فِيهِ .وَهِيَ: إِمَّا حَمْلِيَّةٌ، كَقَوْلِنَا: «زَيْدٌ كَاتِبٌ». وَإِمَّا شَرطِيَّةٌ مُتَّصِلَةٌ، كَقَوْلِنَا: «إِنْ كَانَتِ الشَّمْسُ طَالِعَةً فَالنَّهَارُ مَوْجُودٌ». وَإِمَّا شَرْطِيَّةٌ مُنْفَصِلَةٌ، كَقَوْلِنَا: «الْعَدَدُ إِمَّا زَوْجٌ وَإِمَّا فَرْدٌ». وَالجُزْءُ الْأَوَّلُ مِنَ الحَمْلِيَّةِ يُسَمَّى مَوْضُوعًا، وَالثَّانِي مَحْمُولاً. وَالجُزْءُ الْأَوَّلُ مِنَ الشَّرْطِيَّةِ يُسَمَّى مُقَدَّمًا، وَالثَّانِي تَالِيًا.

[١٧] وَالْقَضِيَّةُ: إِمَّا مُوجِبَةٌ، كَقَوْلِنَا: «زَيْدٌ كَاتِبٌ». وَإِمَّا سَالِبَةٌ، كَقَوْلِنَا: «زَيْدٌ لَيْسَ بِكَاتِبٍ» .وَكُلٌّ وَاحِدَةٍ مِنْهُمَا إِمَّا مَخْصُوصَةٌ كَمَا ذَكَرْنَا، وَإِمَّا كُلِّيَّةٌ مُسَوَّرَةٌ، كَقَوْلِنَا: «كُلُّ إِنْسَانٍ كَاتِبٌ» وَ «لاَ شَيْءَ مِنَ الْإِنْسَانِ بِكَاتِبٍ». وَإِمَّا جُزْئِيَّةٌ مُسَوَّرَةٌ، كَقَوْلِنَا: «بَعْضُ الْإِنْسَانِ كَاتِبٌ» وَ «بَعْضُ الْإِنْسَانِ لَيْسَ بِكَاتِبٍ». وَإِمَّا أَنْ لا يَكُونَ كَذٰلِكَ، وَتُسَمَّى مُهْمَلَةً، كَقَوْلِنَا: «الْإِنْسَانُ كَاتِبٌ» وَ «الْإِنْسَانُ لَيْسَ بِكَاتِبٍ».

[18] Conjunctive [conditional propositions] are either **necessary** (*luzūmiyya*), as in our statement, "if the sun is out then it is daytime" or they are **contingent** (*ittifāqiyya*), as in our statement, "if humans are rational then donkeys bray." The disjunctive [conditional proposition] is either a strong [disjunctive], as in our statement, "numbers are either even or odd," and they (the disjuncts) are simultaneously **mutually exclusive and cannot be collectively false** (*māniʿat al-jamʿ wa-māniʿat al-khuluww*).

[19] Or they are only mutually exclusive, as in our statement, "this thing is either a rock or a tree."

[20] Or they can only be not collectively false, as in our statement, "Zayd is either in the water or he is not drowning."

[21] Disjunctive propositions can also be in three parts, as in our statement, "numbers are either greater [than], lesser [than], or equal [to]."

[١٨] وَالمُتَّصِلَةُ: إِمَّا **لُزُومِيَّةٌ**، كَقَوْلِنَا: «إِنْ كَانَتِ الشَّمْسُ طَالِعَةً فالنَّهَارُ مَوْجُودٌ». وَإِمَّا **اتِّفَاقِيَّةٌ**، كَقَوْلِنَا: «إِنْ كَانَ الْإِنْسَانُ نَاطِقًا فَالْحِمَارُ نَاهِقٌ». وَالمُنْفَصِلَةُ: إِمَّا حَقِيقَةٌ، كَقَوْلِنَا: «الْعَدَدُ إِمَّا زَوْجٌ وَإِمَّا فَرْدٌ». **وَهِيَ مَانِعَةُ الجَمْعِ وَالْخُلُوِّ مَعًا.**

[١٩] وَإِمَّا مَانِعَةُ الجَمْعِ فَقَطْ، كَقَوْلِنَا: «هذَا الشَّيْءُ إِمَّا حَجَرٌ أَوْ شَجَرٌ».

[٢٠] وَإِمَّا مَانِعَةُ الْخُلُوِّ فَقَطْ، كَقَوْلِنَا: «زَيْدٌ إِمَّا أَنْ يَكُونَ فِي الْبَحْرِ وَإِمَّا أَنْ لاَ يَغْرَقَ».

[٢١] وَقَدْ تَكُونُ المُنْفَصِلاَتُ ذَاتَ أَجْزَاءٍ ثَلَاثَةٍ، كَقَوْلِنَا: «الْعَدَدُ إِمَّا زَائِدٌ أَوْ نَاقِصٌ أَوْ مُسَاوٍ».

Opposition

[22] Opposition is a difference between two categorical propositions in [terms of] affirmation or negation such that one of them must be true and the other must be false, as in our statements, "Zayd is a writer" and "Zayd is not a writer." This is not established, except after there is [a complete] equivalence of the subject, predicate, timing, place, relationship, capacity and action, universals and particulars, and conditions.

[23] The [contradictory] opposition of a **universal affirmative proposition** is a **particular negative proposition.** And the [contradictory] opposition of a **universal negative proposition** is **a particular affirmative proposition**, such as our statement: "all humans are animals" and "some humans are not animals." As well as [our statements]: "no human is an animal" and "some humans are animals."

[24] **Two quantified propositions** (*maḥṣūratān*) do not establish a [contradictory] opposition between them except by differing in the [quantity of their] universals and particulars. This is because two universal propositions can both be false, such as our statements, "all humans are writers" and "no humans are writers." [Similarly], two particular propositions can both be true, as in our statements, "some humans are writers" and "some humans are not writers."

التَّنَاقُضُ

[٢٢] هُوَ اخْتِلَافُ الْقَضِيَّتَيْنِ بِالْإِيجَابِ وَالسَّلْبِ بِحَيْثُ يَقْتَضِي لِذَاتِهِ أَنْ تَكُونَ إِحْدَاهُمَا صَادِقَةً وَالْأُخْرَى كَاذِبَةً، كَقَوْلِنَا: «زَيْدٌ كَاتِبٌ».. «زَيْدٌ لَيْسَ بِكَاتِبٍ». وَلَا يَتَحَقَّقُ ذَلِكَ إِلَّا بَعْدَ اتِّفَاقِهِمَا فِي الْمَوْضُوعِ، وَالْمَحْمُولِ، وَالزَّمَانِ، وَالْمَكَانِ، وَالْإِضَافَةِ، وَالْقُوَّةِ وَالْفِعْلِ، وَالْكُلِّ وَالْجُزْءِ، وَالشَّرْطِ.

[٢٣] ونَقِيضُ الْمُوجِبَةِ الْكُلِّيَّةِ إِنَّمَا هُوَ السَّالِبَةُ الْجُزْئِيَّةُ، وَنَقِيضُ السَّالِبَةِ الْكُلِّيَّةِ إِنَّمَا هُوَ الْمُوجِبَةُ الْجُزْئِيَّةُ، كَقَوْلِنَا: «كُلُّ إِنْسَانٍ حَيَوانٌ»....«بَعْضُ الْإِنْسَانِ لَيْسَ بِحَيَوانٍ» و «لَا شَيْءَ مِنَ الْإِنْسَانِ بِحَيَوانٍ»... «بَعْضُ الْإِنْسَانِ حَيَوانٌ».

[٢٤] فالْمَحْصُورَتَانِ لَا يَتَحَقَّقُ التَّنَاقُضُ بَيْنَهُمَا إِلَّا بَعْدَ اخْتِلَافِهِمَا فِي الْكُلِّيَّةِ وَ الْجُزْئِيَّةِ؛ لِأَنَّ الْكُلِّيَّتَيْنِ قَدْ تَكْذِبَانِ، كَقَوْلِنَا: «كُلُّ إِنْسَانٍ كَاتِبٌ» وَ «لَا شَيْءَ مِنَ الْإِنْسَانِ بِكَاتِبٍ»، وَالْجُزْئِيَّتَيْنِ قَدْ تَصْدُقَانِ، كَقَوْلِنَا: «بَعْضُ الْإِنْسَانِ كَاتِبٌ»... «بَعْضُ الْإِنْسَانِ لَيْسَ بِكَاتِبٍ».

Conversion

[25] Conversion (*ʿaks al-mustawī*) [involves] the subject term being made into the predicate term and the predicate term being made into the subject term while maintaining the affirmative or negative [quality of the proposition], and [maintaining its] truth or falsehood. A universal affirmative proposition does not convert to a universal proposition. Although our statement, "every human is an animal" is true, the converse that "every animal is a human" is not true. Therefore, it [i.e., the statement "every animal is a human"] must convert to a particular proposition. This is [true] because if we say, "every human is an animal," it would be accurate [to say], "some animals are humans." [This is true because] we find elements of specific traits in [both] humans and animals. Thus, it is [true] that "some animals are humans."

[26] Based on this reasoning, a particular affirmative proposition is also converted as a particular proposition. A universal negative proposition is converted as a universal proposition. This is self-evident, because if it is true that "no stone is a human," then it is [also] true that "no human is a stone." A particular negative proposition has no necessary conversion [pattern] because our statement, "some animals are not humans," is true, whereas its conversion is not true.

الْعَكْسُ

[٢٥] هُوَ أَنْ يُصَيَّرَ الْمَوْضُوعُ مَحْمُولاً وَالْمَحْمُولُ مَوْضُوعًا مَعَ بَقَاءِ الْإِيجَابِ وَالسَّلْبِ بِحَالِهِ وَالتَّصْدِيقِ وَالتَّكْذِيبِ بِحَالِهِ. الْمُوجِبَةُ الْكُلِّيَّةُ لاَ تَنْعَكِسُ كُلِّيَّةً؛ إِذْ يَصْدُقُ قَوْلُنَا: «كُلُّ إِنْسَانٍ حَيَوَانٌ»، وَلَمْ يَصْدُقْ «كُلُّ حَيَوَانٍ إِنْسَانٌ»، بَل تَنْعَكِسُ جُزْئِيَّةً؛ لِأَنَّا إِذَا قُلْنَا: «كُلُّ إِنْسَانٍ حَيَوَانٌ» يَصْدُقُ: «بَعْضُ الحَيَوَانِ إِنْسَانٌ»، فَإِنَّا نَجِدُ شَيْئًا مُعَيَّنًا مَوْصُوفًا بِالْإِنْسَانِ وَالحَيَوَانِ، فَيَكُونُ «بَعْضُ الحَيَوَانِ إِنْسَانًا».

[٢٦] وَالمُوجِبَةُ الجُزْئِيَّةُ أَيْضًا تَنْعَكِسُ جُزْئِيَّةً بِهَذِهِ الحُجَّةِ. وَالسَّالِبَةُ الْكُلِّيَّةُ تَنْعَكِسُ كُلِّيَّةً، وَذلِكَ بَيِّنٌ فِي نَفْسِهِ، فإِنَّهُ إِذَا صَدَقَ: «لاَ شَيْءَ مِنَ الحَجَرِ بِإِنْسَانٍ» صَدَقَ «لاَ شَيْءَ مِنَ الْإِنْسَانِ بِحَجَرٍ». وَالسَّالِبَةُ الجُزْئِيَّةُ لاَ عَكْسَ لَهَا لُزُومًا؛ لِأَنَّهُ يَصْدُقُ قَوْلُنَا: «بَعْضُ الحَيَوَانِ لَيْسَ بِإِنْسَانٍ» وَلاَ يَصْدُقُ عَكْسُهُ.

Syllogism

[27] [A syllogism] is an assertion composed of [other] assertions, which if accepted as true, necessitates another assertion. It can be a **correlative [syllogism]** (*iqtirānī*), such as our statement: "each body is formed," and "each thing which is formed is temporal" therefore "each body is temporal." Alternatively, it can be a **selective [syllogism]** (*istithnā'ī*), such as our statement, "if the sun is out, then it is daytime." However, "it is not daytime," therefore, "the sun is not out."

[28] What is repeated between the two premises of the syllogism is referred to as the "**middle term**" (*ḥadd awsaṭ*). The subject of the conclusion is referred to as the **minor term** (*ḥadd aṣghar*) and its predicate is the **major term** (*ḥadd akbar*). The premise that contains the minor term is referred to as the **minor** [premise] (*ṣughrā*) and the one that contains the major term is known as the **major** [premise] (*kubrā*). The structural composition of the major and minor premises [of the syllogism] is called a figure (*shakl*).

[29] There are four figures [of syllogisms]. If the middle term is the predicate in the minor premise and the subject in the major premise, then it is the **first figure.** If it is the inversion [of this] then it is the **fourth figure.** If [the middle term] is the subject in both [premises] then it is the **third figure.** If [the middle term] is the predicate in both [premises], then it is the **second figure.** These are the four figures outlined in logic.

الْقِياسُ

[٢٧] هُوَ قَوْلٌ مُؤَلَّفٌ مِنْ أَقْوَالٍ مَتَى سُلِّمَتْ لَزِمَ عَنْهَا لِذَاتِهَا قَوْلٌ آخَرُ. **وَهُوَ إِمَّا اقْتِرَانِيٌّ**، كَقَوْلِنَا: «كُلُّ جِسْمٍ مُؤَلَّفٌ» وَ «كُلُّ مُؤَلَّفٍ مُحْدَثٌ» «فَكُلُّ جِسْمٍ مُحْدَثٌ». **وَإِمَّا اسْتِثْنَائِيٌّ**، كَقَوْلِنَا: «إِنْ كَانَتِ الشَّمْسُ طَالِعَةً فَالنَّهَارُ مَوْجُدٌ»... «لَكِنَّ النَّهَارَ لَيْسَ بِمَوْجُودٍ»... «فَالشَّمْسُ لَيْسَتْ بِطَالِعَةٍ ».

[٢٨] وَالْمُكَرَّرُ بَيْنَ مُقَدِّمَتَي الْقِيَاسِ يُسَمَّى **حَدًّا أَوْسَطَ**، وَمَوْضُوعُ الْمَطْلُوبِ يُسَمَّى **حَدّاً أَصْغَرَ**، وَمَحْمُولُهُ يَسَمَّى **حَدًّا أَكْبَرَ**، وَالْمُقَدِّمَةُ الَّتِي فِيهَا الْأَصْغَرُ تُسَمَّى **صُغْرَى**، وَالَّتِي فِيهَا الْأَكْبَرُ تُسَمَّى **كُبْرَى**، وَهَيْئَةُ التَّأْلِيفِ من الصُّغْرَى و الْكُبْرَى تُسَمَّى **شَكْلاً**.

[٢٩] وَالْأَشْكَالُ أَرْبَعَةٌ؛ لِأَنَّ الحَدَّ الْأَوْسَطَ إِنْ كَانَ مَحْمُولاً فِي الصُّغْرَى مَوْضُوعًا فِي الْكُبْرَى **فَهُوَ الشَّكْلُ الْأَوَّلُ**، وَإِنْ كَانَ بِالْعَكْسِ **فَهُوَ الرَّابِعُ**، وَإِنْ كَانَ مَوْضُوعًا فِيهِمَا **فَهُوَ الثَّالِثُ**، وَإِنْ كَانَ مَحْمُولاً فِيهِمَا **فَهُوَ الثَّانِي**. فَهَذِهِ هِيَ الْأَشْكَالُ الْأَرْبَعَةُ الْمَذْكُورَةُ فِي الْمَنْطِقِ.

[30] The fourth figure is exceedingly distant from what is natural. One with a sound mind and a steady disposition does not need to revert the second [figure] into the first [figure]. The second [figure] is derived when there is a contradiction between the two premises [by way of] either affirmation or negation. The first figure is the one that has been considered the standard for [deductive] knowledge. We presented it here to form a blueprint and derive what is requested.

[There are] four optimal moods

[31] **First:** As in our statement, "each body is formed" and "each thing that has been formed is temporal," therefore, "each body is temporal."

[32] **Second:** As in our statement, "each body is formed," and "nothing that is formed is eternal," therefore "no body is eternal."

[33] **Third:** As in our statement, "some bodies are formed," and "everything that is formed is temporal," therefore "some bodies are temporal."

[34] **Fourth:** As in our statement, "some bodies are formed," and "nothing that is formed is eternal," therefore, "some bodies are not eternal."

[٣٠] وَالشَّكْلُ الرَّابِعُ مِنْهَا بَعِيدٌ عَنِ الطَّبْعِ جِدًّا. والَّذِي له عَقْلٌ سَلِيمٌ وَ طَبْعٌ مُسْتَقِيمٌ لاَ يَحْتَاجُ إِلَى رَدِّ الثَّانِي إِلَى الْأَوَّلِ. وَإِنَّمَا يُنْتِجُ الثَّانِي عِنْدَ اخْتِلاَفِ مُقَدِّمَتَيْهِ بِالْإِيجَابِ وَالسَّلْبِ. وَالشَّكْلُ الْأَوَّلُ هُوَ الَّذِي جُعِلَ مِعْيَارًا لِلْعُلُومِ، فَنُورِدُهُ هَهُنَا لِيُجْعَلَ دُسْتُورًا وَ يُسْتَنْتَجَ مِنْهُ الْمَطْلُوبُ وَضُرُوبُهُ الْمُنْتِجَةُ أَرْبَعَةٌ:

[٣١] الْأَوَّلُ: كَقَوْلِنَا: «كُلُّ جِسْمٍ مُؤَلَّفٌ» وَ «كُلُّ مُؤَلَّفٍ مُحْدَثٌ» «فَكُلُّ جِسْمٍ مُحْدَثٌ».

[٣٢] الثَّانِي: كَقَوْلِنَا: «كُلُّ جِسْمٍ مُؤَلَّفٌ» وَ «لاَ شَيْءَ مِنَ الْمُؤَلَّفِ بِقَدِيمٍ» «فَلاَ شَيْءَ مِنَ الْجِسْمِ بِقَدِيمٍ».

[٣٣] الثَّالِثُ: كَقَوْلِنَا: «بَعْضُ الْجِسْمِ مُؤَلَّفٌ» وَ «كُلُّ مُؤَلَّفٍ حَادِثٌ» «فَبَعْضُ الْجِسْمِ حَادِثٌ».

[٣٤] الرَّابِعُ: كَقَوْلِنَا: «بَعْضُ الْجِسْمِ مُؤَلَّفٌ» وَ «لاَ شَيْءَ مِنَ الْمُؤَلَّفِ بِقَدِيمٍ» «فَبَعْضُ الْجِسْمِ لَيْسَ بِقَدِيمٍ».

[35] **Correlative syllogisms** (*iqtirānī*) are composed of two categorical propositions, as encountered.

[36] Or they are composed of two conjunctive [propositions], as in our statement, "if the sun is out then it is daytime," and "every time it is daytime, the earth is illuminated," therefore, "if the sun is out, the earth is illuminated."

[37] Alternatively, a [correlative syllogism] can be composed of two disjunctive [propositions], as in our statement, "every [whole] number is either even or odd," and "every even number is either the pair of a pair or a pair of an odd number," therefore, "every number is either odd or a pair of a pair or the pair of an odd number."

[38] It can also be composed of a categorical (*ḥamliyya*) [proposition] and a conjunctive proposition, as in our statement, "as long as this [being] is a human then he is [also] an animal," and "every animal is a body," therefore, "every being that is a human is also a body."

[39] Or it can be composed of a categorical [proposition] and a disjunctive proposition, as in our statement, "each number is either even or odd," and "each even [number] can then be divided into two equals," therefore, "each number is either odd, or can be divided into two equals."

[40] Or it is composed of a conjunctive [proposition] and disjunctive [proposition], as in our statement, "as long as this [being] is a human then he is an animal," and "every animal is either white or black," therefore, "as long as this [being] is a human then he is either white or black."

[٣٥] **وَالِاقْتِرَانِيُّ**: إِمَّا مُرَكَّبٌ مِنْ حَمْلِيَّتَيْنِ كَمَا مَرَّ.

[٣٦] وَإِمَّا مِنْ مُتَّصِلَتَيْنِ، كَقَوْلِنَا: «إِنْ كَانَتِ الشَّمْسُ طَالِعَةً فَالنَّهَارُ مَوْجُودٌ» وَ «كُلَّمَا كَانَ النَّهَارُ مَوْجُودًا فَالْأَرْضُ مُضِيئَةٌ» يُنْتِجُ: «إِنْ كَانَتِ الشَّمْسُ طَالِعَةً فَالْأَرْضُ مُضِيئَةٌ».

[٣٧] وَإِمَّا مِنْ مُنْفَصِلَتَيْنِ، كَقَوْلِنَا: «كُلُّ عَدَدٍ فَهُوَ إِمَّا زَوْجٌ أَوْ فَرْدٌ» وَ «كُلُّ زَوْجٍ فَهُوَ إِمَّا زَوْجُ الزَّوْجِ، أَوْ زَوْجُ الْفَرْدِ» يَنْتُجُ: «كُلُّ عَدَدٍ إِمَّا فَرْدٌ أَوْ زَوْجُ الزَّوْجِ، أَوْ زَوْجُ الْفَرْدِ».

[٣٨] وَإِمَّا مِنْ حَمْلِيَّةٍ وَ مُتَّصِلَةٍ، كَقَوْلِنَا: «كُلَّمَا كَانَ هَذَا إِنْسَانًا فَهُوَ حَيَوَانٌ» وَ «كُلُّ حَيَوَانٍ جِسْمٌ» يَنْتُجُ: «كُلَّمَا كَانَ هَذَا إِنْسَانًا فَهُوَ جِسْمٌ».

[٣٩] وَإِمَّا مِنْ حَمْلِيَّةٍ وَ مُنْفَصِلَةٍ، كَقَوْلِنَا: «كُلُّ عَدَدٍ إِمَّا زَوْجٌ وَ إِمَّا فَرْدٌ» وَ «كُلُّ زَوْجٍ فَهُوَ مُنْقَسِمٌ بِمُتَسَاوِيَيْنِ» يَنْتُجُ: «كُلُّ عَدَدٍ هُوَ إِمَّا فَرْدٌ، أَوْ مُنْقَسِمٌ بِمُتَسَاوِيَيْنِ».

[٤٠] وَإِمَّا مِنْ مُتَّصِلَةٍ وَ مُنْفَصِلَةٍ، كَقَوْلِنَا: «كُلَّمَا كَانَ هَذَا إِنْسَانًا فَهُوَ حَيَوَانٌ» وَ «كُلُّ حَيَوَانٍ إِمَّا أَبْيَضُ وَ إِمَّا أَسْوَدُ». يَنْتُجُ: «كُلَّمَا كَانَ هَذَا إِنْسَانًا فَهُوَ إِمَّا أَبْيَضُ أَوْ أَسْوَدُ».

[41] As for the **selective syllogism**, (*al-qiyās al-istithnāʾī*) the conditional [proposition] is the major premise in it. If [the conditional syllogism] is **conjunctive**, then the [affirmative] selection of the antecedent results in the [affirmation of the] consequent itself. [This is according to] our saying, "if this is a human then he is an animal. He is a human. Therefore, he is an animal." And the selection of a negation of the consequent results in the negation of the antecedent. [This is according to] our saying, "if this is a human then he is an animal. He is not an animal. Therefore, he is not a human."

[42] If it is a strong (*ḥaqīqiyya*) **disjunctive syllogism**, the [affirmative] selection of one of the opposing two disjuncts results in the negation of the other and the selection of the negation of one [of the two opposing disjuncts] results in the affirmation of the other.

[٤١] **وَأَمَّا القِيَاسُ الاسْتِثْنَائِيُّ**: فَالشَّرْطِيَّةُ المَوْضُوعَةُ فِيْهِ إِذَا كَانَتْ **مُتَّصِلَةً**: فَاسْتِثْنَاءُ عَيْنِ المُقَدَّمِ يُنْتِجُ عَيْنَ التَّالِي، كَقَولِنَا: «إِنْ كَانَ هَذَا إِنْسَانًا فَهُوَ حَيَوَانٌ»...«لَكِنَّهُ إِنْسَانٌ» «فهُوَ حيَوَانٌ». واستِثْنَاءُ نَقِيضِ التَّالِي يُنْتِجُ نَقِيْضَ المُقَدَّمِ، كَقَوْلِنَا: «إِنْ كَانَ هَذَا إِنْسَانًا فَهُوَ حَيَوَانٌ»...«لَكِنَّهُ لَيسَ بِحَيَوَانٍ» «فلا يكونُ إِنْسَانًا».

[٤٢] وَإِنْ كانَتْ **مُنْفَصِلَةً حَقِيقِيَّةً**: فَاسْتِثْنَاءُ عَيْنِ أَحَدِ الجُزْئَيْنِ يُنْتِجُ نَقِيْضَ الآخر، وَاسْتِثْنَاءُ نَقِيْضِ أَحدِهِمَا يُنْتِجُ عَيْنَ الآخر.

The Five Syllogistic Arts

[43] **Demonstration** (*burhān*) is a [type of] syllogism comprised of apodictic premises [from which] to derive certain conclusions.

[44] **Apodictic premises are divided into six categories**

[45] (1) **Axioms** (*awwaliyyāt*) like our statement, "one is half of two" or "the whole is greater than its parts."

[46] (2) **Observational Propositions** (*mushāhadāt*) like our statement, "the sun is bright," and "fire burns."

[47] (3) **Empirical Propositions** (*mujarrabāt*) like our statement, "drinks made of bindweed alleviate yellow bile."

[48] (4) **Intuitive Premises** (*ḥadsiyyāt*) like our statement, "the light of the moon is derived from the light of the sun."

[49] (5) **Recurrent mass transmitted** (*tawātur*) **reports** like our statement, "Muḥammad ﷺ proclaimed his prophecy," and "miracles were performed by his hand."

[50] (6) [**Innate Premises** (*fiṭriyyāt*)] are assertions that include syllogisms that must naturally accompany them because of a preconceived intermediate [principle] already present in the mind. For example, [we say] "four is an even [number]," because of the preconception that it [four] can be divided into two equal parts.

الصِّنَاعَاتُ الخَمسُ

[٤٣] **الْبُرْهَانُ** هُوَ قِيَاسٌ مُؤَلَّفٌ مِنْ مُقَدِّمَاتٍ يَقِينِيةٍ لِإِنْتَاجِ الْيَقِيْنِ.

[٤٤] **وَالْيَقِيْنِيَّاتُ سِتَّةُ أَقْسَامٍ:**

[٤٥] ١ - **أَوَلِيَّاتٌ**: كَقَوْلِنَا: «الوَاحِدُ نِصْفُ الاِثْنَيْنِ» وَ «الْكُلُّ أَعْظَمُ مِنَ الجُزْءِ».

[٤٦] ٢ - **وَمُشَاهَدَاتٌ**: كَقَوْلِنَا: «الشَّمْسُ مُشْرِقَةٌ»، وَ «النَّارُ مُحْرِقَةٌ».

[٤٧] ٣ - **وَمُجَرَّبَاتٌ**: كَقَوْلِنَا: «شُرْبُ السَّقَمُونِيَا يُسَهِّلُ الصَّفْرَاءَ».

[٤٨] ٤ - **وَحَدْسِيَّاتٌ**: كَقَوْلِنَا: «نُورُ الْقَمَرِ مُسْتَفَادٌ مِنَ الشَّمْسِ».

[٤٩] ٥ - **وَمُتَوَاتِرَاتٌ**: كَقَوْلِنَا: «مُحَمَّدٌ عَلَيْهِ الصَّلَاةُ وَالسَّلَامُ ادَّعَى النّبُوَّةَ، وَأَظْهَرَ المُعْجِزَةَ عَلى يَدِهِ».

[٥٠] ٦ - **وَقَضَايَا قِيَاسَاتُهَا مَعَهَا**: كَقَوْلِنَا: «الْأَرْبَعَةُ زَوْجٌ» بِسَبَبِ وَسَطٍ حَاضِرٍ فِي الذِّهْنِ وَهُوَ الاِنْقِسَامُ بِمُتَسَاوِيَيْنِ.

[51] **Dialectic** (*jadal*) is a syllogism composed of premises that are commonly accepted [as true].

[52] **Rhetoric** (*khaṭāba*) is a syllogism composed of premises accepted from a credible individual or [one whose opinions] are preferred.

[53] **Poetics** (*shiʿr*) are syllogisms composed of premises that bring joy to the heart or [cause it to] contract.

[54] **Sophistry** (*mughālaṭa*) are syllogisms composed of false premises that resemble the truth or commonly accepted [matters], or [they could be composed of] premises [based on] delusions [or superstitions] (*wahm*).

[55] The reliable [syllogism, in terms of accuracy and truth] is that of **demonstrative** [proofs] (*burhān*), nothing else. This is the end of the epistle on logic.

[٥١] **وَالجَدَلُ:** وَهُوَ قِيَاسٌ مُؤَلَّفٌ مِن مُقَدِّمَاتٍ مَشْهُورَةٍ.

[٥٢] **وَالخَطَابَةُ:** وَهِيَ قِيَاسٌ مُؤَلَّفٌ مِنْ مُقَدِّمَاتٍ مَقْبُولَةٍ مِنْ شَخْصٍ مُعْتَقَدٍ فِيهِ، أَوْ مَظْنُونَةٍ.

[٥٣] **وَالشِّعْرُ:** وَهُوَ قِيَاسٌ مُؤَلَّفٌ مِنْ مُقَدِّمَاتٍ تَنْبَسِطُ مِنْهَا النَّفْسُ أَوْ تَنْقَبِضُ.

[٥٤] **وَالْمُغَالَطَةُ:** وَهِيَ قِيَاسٌ مُؤَلَّفٌ مِنْ مَقَدِّمَاتٍ كَاذِبَةٍ شَبِيهَةٍ بِالْحَقِّ أَوْ بِالْمَشْهُورِةِ، أَوْ مِنْ مُقَدِّمَاتٍ وَهْمِيَّةٍ كَاذِبَةٍ.

[٥٥] وَالْعُمْدَةُ هُوَ الْبُرْهَانُ لاَ غَيْرُ. وَلِيَكُنْ هَذَا آخِرَ الرِّسَالَةِ فِي الْمَنْطِقِ.

شَرْحُ الرِسَالَة

Explanatory Notes on the Primer

Translation

The Logic of Athīr al-Dīn al-Abharī

[1] The shaykh, erudite *imām*, best of the post-classical [scholars], model for the rooted philosophers, Athīr al-Dīn al-Abharī, may God make his resting place pleasant and make paradise his final abode, said: "We thank God the exalted for granting success, ask Him for guidance on His path, and we send prayers upon Muḥammad and the entirety of his kin."

[2] To proceed, this is a treatise on logic. We have conveyed in it what must be understood in order to begin studying any part of the sciences while depending on God, as He is the most generous source of goodness and abundance.

Explanatory Notes

In beginning to read classical texts, it is not uncommon for many to hasten through what is known as the *basmala, ḥamdala,* and *ṣalwala.* This standard format appears at the beginning of classical texts; it is composed of an invocation of God (*basmala*; lit., "in the name of God"), an expression of gratitude to God (*ḥamdala*; lit., "praise be to God"), and sending blessings on the Prophet Muḥammad (*ṣalwala*; lit., "may the peace and blessings of God be on him"). Notably, no two texts have an identical *ḥamdala* and *ṣalwala*. The *ḥamdala*s and *ṣalwala*s of classical texts served at least two functions. First, in many ways they are analogous to a modern ISBN number, and can be a way of distinguishing texts. Encyclopedic lists of books like that of the renowned Ottoman scholar Katip Çelebi often list the *ḥamdala* and *ṣalwala* of a text to clarify a work's identity. Second, the *ḥamdala*s and *ṣalwala*s of a text often serve as a signature or "fingerprint" of the authors themselves. In this segment of a text, the author often used words and phrases that indicate his stream of thought or his position on a controversial theological matter. There are often poetic wordplays and other clues that indicate the author's intent in writing the text. In some ways, these parts of premodern texts resemble the preface of a modern text, in the sense that both reveal information about the author's perspective and rationale in writing a book.

The invocations in the introduction of this text are notably brief, as compared to that of others works (in general). The transmitter of the text gives Athīr al-Dīn al-Abharī titles such as, "the polymath (*ʿallāma*) and foremost scholar of the post-classical era." This indicates that al-Abharī was respected enough in stature to receive the honorific title *ʿallāma*, which is used to refer to those with extensive erudition in a variety of fields of knowledge. The term *mutaʾakhkhirīn* indicates that the followers of al-Abharī recognized a clear distinction between the classical (*mutaqaddimīn*) Ashʿarī theologians who maintained al-Juwaynī's model of theology and the post-classical (*mutaʾakhkhirīn*) Ashʿarī theologians who followed the blueprint of al-Rāzī, whose discussions of theology restructured *kalām* texts to address questions raised by ancient philosophy, as discussed in the introduction. The next phrase, "the model for the rooted philosophers," seems to be a response to those who objected to the study of philosophy on religious grounds. His being "rooted" (*rāsikhīn*) asserts al-Abharī's foundational place in mainstream Islamic theology.

Another noteworthy element of this invocation is al-Abharī's statement that his treatise in logic is intended as a primer for those who wish to study other Islamic (sciences). This statement is designed to remind readers of the importance of logic as a tool to comprehend other fields, such as jurisprudence (*fiqh*) and theology. He also reminds the reader that ultimately, success in the study of logic is achieved through divine facilitation. This is a significant illustration of the harmony that existed between faith and reason, or what we may call "religion and science," in the Islamic intellectual tradition. Invoking God in works that we describe as related to science and reason was a normative practice in classical Islamic texts, whose writers themselves were most often devout Muslims.[1]

1 Note that the Islamic world never experienced a split between the divine and mundane worlds, or between religious/spiritual matters and science, knowledge, philosophy, etc. and therefore, in this sense, cannot be compared to European intellectual traditions.

Translation

Isagoge

[3] Utterances that signify [meanings] by designating meaning to each articulated sound (*bi-l-waḍʿi*) can denote these meanings for which they [the utterances] have been posited, [either] in their entirety through a **full correlation** (*bi-l-muṭābaqa*); or [they can do so] in part through **inclusion** (*bi-l-taḍammun*), if [the meaning that an utterance refers to] is part [of this expression]; or [an utterance can designate a meaning through] what is associated (*yulāzimuhu*) with it in the mind. For example, [the word] "human" refers to a rational animal through full correlation, [and "human" refers] to one of the two categories [i.e., animal or rational being] through inclusion, and ["human" refers to one who is] inclined toward learning and the art of writing through **association** (*bi-l-iltizām*).

Explanatory Notes

Al-Abharī begins his introduction to logic by analyzing what constitutes an utterance (*lafẓ*) that has meaning and by examining how these meanings are conveyed. First, an utterance can convey meaning by being an exact equivalent of what that utterance refers to. Al-Abharī refers to this form of conveying meaning as full correlation (*muṭābaqa*). In the example provided in this text, a rational animal is said to be an exact definition of a human. This definition excludes anything that is not a human and includes all humans. Such an utterance is the most precise form of referring to something.

Second, a word can convey meaning through another word that includes what is being referred to, but is not precise enough to exclude other things that are not being referred to in its categories. Thus, in al-Abharī's example, if rather than saying humans are "rational animals," we say that they are "rational beings," or that they are "animals," it would still refer to humans. However, these broader categories do not restrict the meaning by linking the words "rational" and "animal" in one phrase because they may include other things that are not human. This makes the utterance a less precise way of referring to its object, which in this case is humans.

Finally, an utterance can refer to an object indirectly by causing the mind to form an association with the actual object the utterance indicates. This necessary association is what is known as *iltizām.*[2] Al-Abharī gives an example of this way of conveying meaning by referring to a human as "one who is inclined toward learning and the art of writing." Only one being normally comes to mind from this description, namely, a human.

Another example of the three ways in which utterances can create meanings that refer to something follows here. For example, if we say "Zaynab" we are referring to a specific individual. Here the word "Zaynab" is exact in its reference to a specific person. This is al-Abharī's exact correlation. Alternatively, we could refer to Zaynab by saying, "a woman." While this is an accurate statement, its lack of specificity means that it can include other women who are not Zaynab; al-Abharī refers to this as definition by partial inclusion. Finally, Zaynab could be

2 When Aristotle's tripartite theory of meaning as consisting of sounds, thoughts, and things took hold among logicians in the Arabic speaking world, it was met with resistance from Arabic grammarians who maintained Arabic conceptions of linguistic forms based on oral tradition. For more on the tripartite versus bi-partite debates in early Islamic history, see Peter Adamson and Alexander Key, "Philosophy of Language in the Medieval Arabic Tradition," in *Linguistic Meaning: New Essays in the History of the Philosophy of Language*, ed. Margaret Cameron and Robert J. Stainton (Oxford: Oxford University Press, 2015), 74–99.

referred to by association; for example, we could say, "the professor of theology" or "the woman seated in the front of the classroom." These ways of describing Zaynab directly refer to her by mental associations that cause the listener to infer that we are referring to Zaynab who is a professor of theology and the woman sitting at the front of the classroom.

Concepts (*taṣawwurāt*) and Assents (*taṣdīqāt*) in the Islamic Logic Tradition

The division of logic into sections related to concepts and those related to assents is a unique feature that evolved in the Islamic intellectual tradition of philosophy and post-classical theology (*kalām*). Though this dichotomy first appeared in al-Fārābī's writings (specifically, at the beginning of *al-Burhān*), it was Ibn Sīnā who substantively restructured the contents of Aristotle's *Organon* into aspects of logic that are based on concepts (*taṣawwurāt*) and assents (*taṣdīqāt*);[3] this is portrayed in the sections on logic in his *Ḥikmat al-mashriqiyya* and the *Ishārāt wa-tanbīhāt.*

Al-Abhari's *Isagoge* follows this dichotomy by dividing its discussion on logic into two main sections: concepts and assents; each of these sections has two subsections (mentioned below). The foundations of concepts (*mabādi' al-taṣawwurāt*) includes sections on utterances (*lafẓ*), the five predicables, and definitions. This is followed by a section on the objective of these concepts (*maqāṣid al-taṣawwurāt*), namely, the expository statement (*qawlun shāriḥ*). All of these are various

3 The term "assent" means to agree, especially after deliberation. In logic, judgments are acts of the mind, in which a subject and predicate are equated to produce propositions. Inferences are the process of combining premises in the form of propositions to arrive at a conclusion. The term *taṣdīq* is used in Arabic logic such that it includes judgments (made by identifying *qaḍāya*) and inferences (made by identifying *qiyās*). Since no single term in English logic fully correlates to this use of *taṣdīqāt* in Arabic logic, we translate it as "assents."

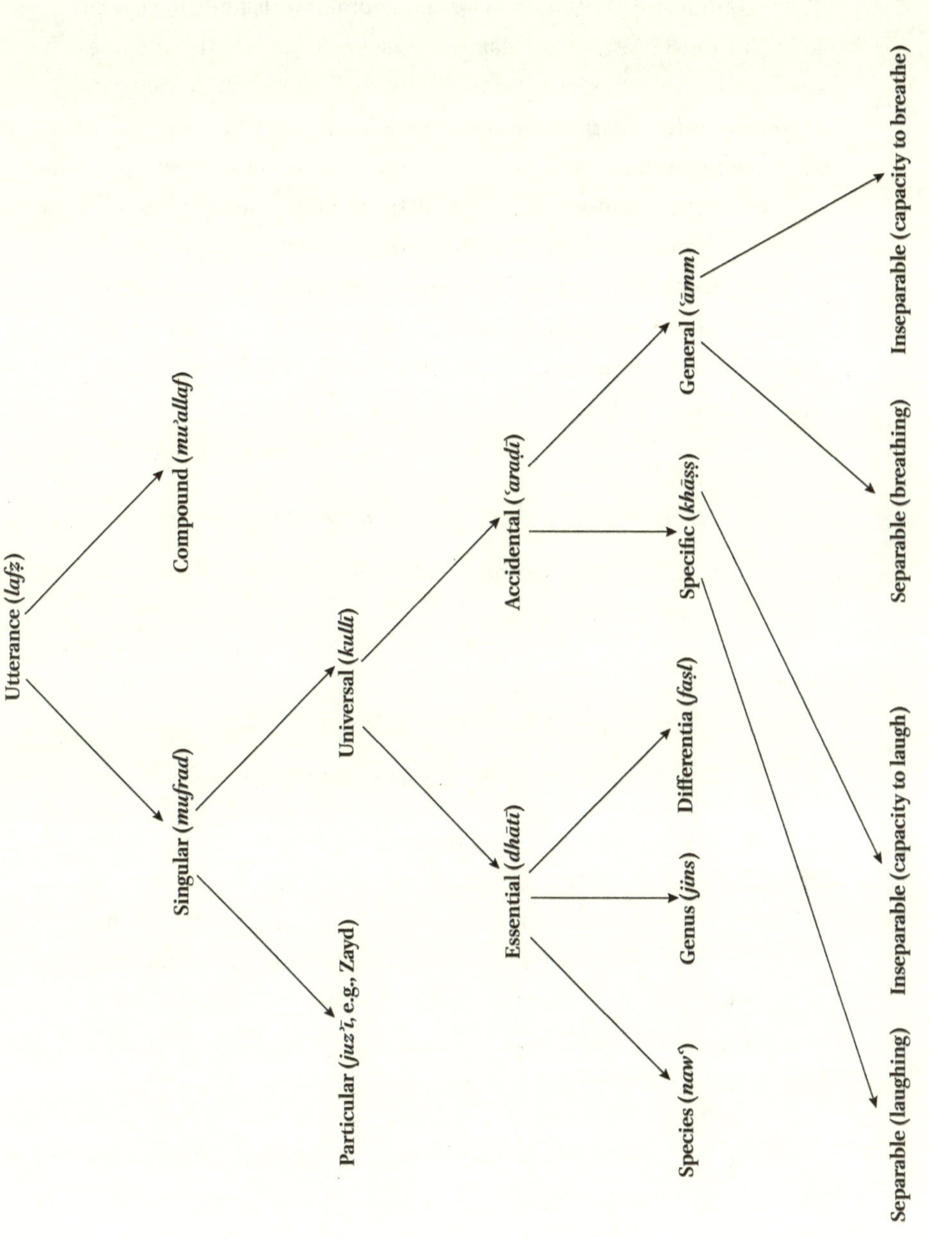

Diagram 1: Divisons of Utterances

aspects of concepts that are the building blocks for making assents. The second segment of the *Isagoge* (and numerous Islamic logic texts following Ibn Sīnā's model) deals with assents (*taṣdīqāt*); this includes the foundations of assents (*mabādi' al-taṣdīqāt*) and discussions on propositions (*qaḍāya*). The second segment on assents includes what later commentators categorized as the objectives of assents (*maqāṣid al-taṣdīqāt*); these objectives include all the ways that new propositions and a conclusion can be derived directly or indirectly (*istidlāl mubāshir wa-ghayr mubāshir*) from the foundational propositions. These include conversion (*'aks*), opposition (*tanāquḍ*), syllogisms (*qiyās*), and the five syllogistic arts (*al-ṣina'āt al-khams*) at the end of al-Abharī's *Isagoge*. This division of concepts and assents is outlined below.

1. Concepts
    a. foundations of concepts (*mabādi' al-taṣawwurāt*)
    b. objectives of conceptual foundations (*maqāṣid al-taṣawwurāt*)
2. Assents
    a. foundations of assents (*mabādi' al-taṣdīqāt*)
    b. objectives of assents (*maqāṣid al-taṣdīqāt*)

This model of dividing logic texts topically was later solidified through the work of Fakhr al-Dīn al-Rāzī, who merged theology with philosophy using some of the structural frameworks and divisions set by Ibn Sīnā. Post-classical Muslim theologians who came after al-Rāzī, like al-Bayḍāwī, Sharīf al-Jurjānī, al-Taftazānī, Ismail Gelenbevi, Mullā al-Fanārī, 'Alī al-Qushjī (d. 879/1474), Shams al-Dīn al-Iṣfahānī, Sirāj al-Dīn al-Urmawī, al-Khunajī (d. 646/1248) and many others further developed a sophisticated discourse around matters of epistemology, a discourse that came to epitomize Muslim philosophical theologians of the seventh/thirteenth to twelfth/eighteenth centuries. When Meno's famous paradox of inquiry led to philosophical debates about the nature of knowledge, Muslim thinkers were at the forefront of developing the field of epistemology in the framework of Islamic thought and were keenly interested in the implications this discussion posed in relation to the ability to know God and His laws.

For the purposes of understanding the *Isagoge*, concepts and assents can be explained simply. Concepts are bits of knowledge that pre-exist in our minds without our having to do any research. They could be matters that are self-evident in the sense that one knows them to be true without question, such as the sky is blue or fire is hot. Or, they could be acquired at some point in our lives (like the heat of fire), but once acquired, they are stored in our minds. Muslim thinkers argued that a foundation of concepts must exist in our minds in order to build new knowledge. Otherwise, without foundational concepts in the mind that serve as building blocks for further knowledge, the problem of infinite regress (*tasalsul*) arises; that is, the process in which one looks for a premise for another premise for another premise *ad infinitum* before any new conclusions can be drawn about anything. Al-Abharī's section on utterances, definitions, and expository statements deals with aspects of concepts (*taṣawwurāt*).

Assents (*taṣdīqāt*) utilize information in the form of concepts to create correlations between these concepts, and these correlations lead to new information. Assents can take the form of propositional statements, in which a predicate is distributed to a subject. In English logic, these are known as **judgments.** Assents can also take the form of syllogisms that form correlations between axiomatic premises that are pre-established as true. In English logic, this is known as **inference.** In both cases we see that concepts are the building blocks through which assents are derived.

Translation

[4] **Expressions** are either **singular** (*mufrad*), such as the word "human" (*insān*), which does not convey a partial meaning if it were divided into two parts [such as *in* and *sān*]. Or they [expressions] can be compound (*mu'allaf*), such as [the expression] "rock thrower."

Explanatory Notes

A singular word (*mufrad*) is a meaningful expression that cannot be further divided into more words that have meaning. For example, "garden" is a singular word. We cannot divide the word "garden" into "gar" and "den." Other examples include words such as computer, table, and factory.[4]

By contrast, a compound word is composed of other words and potentially can be divided into words that have independent meanings. In English grammar, compound words are categorized as being open, closed, or hyphenated. Examples of open compound words include ice cream, real estate, high school, and full moon. Examples of closed compound words include grandmother, sunflower, footprint, and grasshopper. Examples of hyphenated compound words include part-time, long-term, and high-tech. Al-Abharī provides the example of the compound word "rock thrower." This word can be divided further into "rock" and "thrower."

4 For further reading, see Shams Inati, "Ibn Sina on Single Expressions," in *Islamic Theology and Philosophy: Studies in Honor of George Hourani*, ed. Michael E. Marmura (Albany: State University of New York Press, 1984), 148–159.

TRANSLATION

[5] A singular expression can be either **universal** (*kullī*), which is [an expression] that does not impede the conception of its meaning being shared among many, like the term "human." Or it can be a **particular** (*juz'ī*) [expression], which means it is an expression that prevents the conception of its meaning [being shared by many], like [for instance], "Zayd."

EXPLANATORY NOTES

A universal (*kullī*) expression is one that can be applied to a number of different things. For example, the term "human" is universal in that Zaynab, 'Ā'isha, and Zachary can all be included in this property of shared "humanity." A particular (*juz'ī*) expression is a type of expression that cannot be applied to a number of other things. In al-Abharī's example, the word "Zayd" refers to a specific person. This makes the word "Zayd" a particular expression. By contrast, the word "human" can refer to many people, including Zayd. Thus, it is a universal expression.

Translation

[6] Furthermore, a **universal** [expression] is either **essential** (*dhātī*), which means it constitutes the essential nature of each of [the] particulars [included in this universal term], such as [the word] "animal" in relation to "human" and "horse." Or [a universal expression] is **accidental** (*ʿaraḍī*), which means it contradicts this [principle mentioned above], such as laughing in relation to humans.[5]

Explanatory Notes

Substances and Accidents: *Jawhar, dhāt,* and *ʿaraḍ*

Muslim philosophers classified the modes of being into that of *jawhar, dhāt,* and *ʿaraḍ.* Ibn Sīnā devoted a significant proportion of his writing to the topic of existence (*wujūd*) as it pertains to God, the universe, and the world. The various arguments for the existence of God were presented in different ways by a vast number of philosophical theologians or *kalām* specialists who built on the ideas presented by Ibn Sīnā in his *Shifāʾ*. In al-Abharī's treatise on logic, he introduces the concepts of substances and accidents as he would to a beginning student in the field of Islamic studies.

This theory of the way things can exist is rooted in Aristotelian logic, which states that all things can either exist "in themselves" or must depend on the existence of another entity in order to "exist in others." Things like humans, trees, and cars can be considered to exist

5 Laughing can be a quality of some humans but it is not essential to their humanity and therefore it is an accident (*ʿaraḍ*).

in themselves without depending on the existence of another thing to make them exist. This is known as a primary substance (*jawhar*). Entities such as "red," "fifty pounds," and "small" must have another object in which they exist. A shirt can be red, a boy can be fifty pounds, and a car can be small. None of these things can exist independently in themselves. It is not possible to see fifty pounds walking down a street or red floating around a room. Their existence is dependent on the substance that they inhabit. Such properties that are dependent on a substance to exist are called accidents (*ʿaraḍ*).

Substances are also divided into two types: Primary and secondary. Primary substances are the specific individual things that are being referred to, such as Zayd. Secondary substances are universal properties that give a thing its intrinsic nature. The secondary substance of Zayd is humanity. It is a shared idea that people have, that makes a car still a car, or makes a man still a man, despite their various accidents, like shape, color, and appearance. This shared "carness," "manness," "animalness," "treeness," etc. are known as secondary substances (*dhāt*). These secondary substances are also the *essence* of things, that is, this is what gives them their identity and makes them what they are (*māhiya*). The essence that makes a thing what it is, is referred to as "quiddity," which is the usual translation of *māhiya*. Hence, in English texts, the words *dhāt* and essence (which can be another aspect of an object's "whatness" or quiddity) are often used interchangeably. In later studies in metaphysics and theology, we can see that theologians and philosophers emphasize the terms *dhāt* and *māhiya* in different ways to describe the existences of substances. While all of this may seem obscure to a non-specialist, understanding these concepts is essential to reading later theological texts that discuss topics such as the oneness of God, God's attributes, and the relationship of the world to the divine.

The Ten Categories of Being (*maqūlāt*)

The ten categories of being are intellectual tools we can use to think about topics related to Islamic philosophy and theology. These categories originated in the works of Ibn Sīnā, who utilized Aristotle's writings in his *Categories* to list the ways in which a substance or accidents can be said to exist (*maqūlāt*).[6] The Arabic term *maqūlāt* comes from the root q-w-l which means to speak (*maqūlāt* should not be confused with the term *maʿqūlāt*, which refers to another concept known as intelligibles).

The first of the ten categories by which to describe something as existing is as a substance. The other nine categories describe ways that accidents can exist based on their relationship to a substance. The ten categories are as follows.

1. **Substance (*jawhar*):** "Whatness" (*māhiya*) or the essence of an object. This is what makes it what it is.

2. **Quantity (*kammiyya*):** How many? How much? For example, when we say "two apples," two is an accident whose existence is dependent on the existence of the apples, which are substances.

3. **Quality (*kayfiyya*):** This is the qualification of a thing that includes accidents such as a state (pleasant), color (red), and shape (square).

4. **Relation (*iḍāfa*):** This is the relational connections between objects; for example, on top of, after, or before.

5. **Action (*fiʿl*):** This specifies what a substance is doing; for example, walking, talking, or praying.

6. **Affective (*infiʿāl*):** This is what is being done to a substance; for example, being pressured, broken, or mended.

7. **Location (*makān*):** This is the place where a substance is located; for example, at school, in the United States, or in a car.

---

6 Early Arab logicians used the Greek term *kateguryas* in Arabic (in their translation of Aristotle's *Categories*). Al-Fārābī translated the term as *maqūlāt* ("that which can be said of something").

8. **Position (*waḍʿ*):** This refers to the way a substance is positioned; for example, flat, sitting, lying down, resting, or upright.
9. **Time (*zamān*):** This refers to when a substance is doing something; for example, walking in the morning, or arriving in an hour.
10. **Possession (*mulkiyya*):** This is the relation of an object to another with regard to possession; for example, ʿĀʾisha's raincoat.

Essential (*dhātī*) and Accidental (*ʿaraḍī*) Properties

A universal (*kullī*) word used to describe a thing can be a property that is essential (*dhātī*) to its identity as that thing or it can be a property that is incidental (i.e., not essential to its identity). The non-essential properties are referred to as "accidents" (*ʿaraḍ*). For example, although the property of being human is universal, in that it can be applied to a wide range of people, it is still essential to Zayd being who he is. If Zayd were not human, he could not be Zayd. By contrast, laughing is an "accidental" property, in that it is not essential to Zayd's identity that he laugh. Humans are distinguished from other animals in that they have the capacity (*quwwa*) to laugh and actually do laugh. However, laughing is not an essential property that defines one's humanity, it is an accidental (or perhaps a functionally incidental) property. If Zayd never laughed, he would still be Zayd.

TRANSLATION

[7] The **essential** can be used as an answer to what something is in terms of a [broadly] shared identity, such as the term animal in relation to humans and horses. And this is [called] a **genus** (*jins*). [A genus] is described as a universal [property] that can be said of a variety of entities that differ in their true natures, [in] answer to [the question] of what it is.

[8] Alternatively, a [term] with both shared and specialized [properties] can be said to be an answer to the question, "what is it." For example, [one might use the word] "human" in reference to both Zayd and ʿAmr. This is [called] the **species** (*nawʿ*). It is described as a universal [term] that can be applied to numerous entities that do not differ in their true nature, [in] answer to [the question], of what it is.

[9] Or it could be that [one is not] responding [to the question] "what is it," but is instead responding to [the question] "what thing is it, in its essence?" This is what distinguishes it from other things it shares a genus with, such as [the quality of being] rational, in regard to humans. This is called **differentia** (*faṣl*). It is described as a universal [property] that refers to an entity [in] answer to [the question] of "what is it in essence."

Explanatory Notes

The Five Predicables (*kulliyāt al-khams*)

The *Isagoge* includes discussions about what are known as the five predicables (Latin, *quinque voces*) of traditional logic. The five predicables describe the five ways in which one can refer to something; these ultimately lead to a definition of that entity. These are different from categories, because categories list what (time, quantity, quality) can be said to describe a subject, rather than ways of referring to the same thing—ways that are necessary to *define it*. The five predicables are genus (*jins*), species (*nawʿ*), differentia (*faṣl*), property (*khāṣṣa*), and accident (*ʿaraḍ ʿāmm*). Both "property" and "accident" are considered accidental universals for reasons that are explained later.

For example, if we ask, how can we refer to Zayd, we could say that he is an animal or we could be more specific and say that he is a human or we could be even more specific and say that he is a boy, and so on by adding specific accidents to help the listener identify the particular animal who is a human, who is a boy, who is Zayd. This can be confusing because in common language, these too can be described as "categories"—in this case they are categories of specificity. Each of these general and more specific ways of describing Zayd reflect *how* we can refer to Zayd. In Arabic logic these five predicables are known as the "five universals" (*kulliyāt al-khams*). This is because each of the five predicables refers to a universal framework that is shared with other groups (as in genus, species, and differentia) or to accidents that are composed of universal properties that can apply specifically to the entity referenced.

The question "what is it" (*mā huwa*) originally developed from the heuristic inquiry methods proposed by Aristotle in his *Posterior Analytics*; Ibn Sīnā later expanded on these methods in his *Shifāʾ*.[7]

---

7 Aristotle challenged his teacher Plato's theory of knowledge which divided ways of knowing into that which is visible vs. that which is intelligible.

Muslim thinkers have examined, among other questions, the connection between existence (*wujūd*) and its "whatness" or quiddity (*māhiya*). The quiddity (or lack thereof) of God's existence (*wujūd*) in contrast to human existence is a foundational matter of debate in Islamic theology (*kalām*) and its conception of Islamic monotheism.

Thus, we see al-Abharī identifying what makes something what it is by describing shared traits of similar objects; these in turn portray the cognitive frameworks by which a specific thing is known (that is, through its different forms of affiliation with each of the five predicables). For instance, humans and horses are both animals (a genus) because they share the quality of being living beings (unlike clouds or rocks). Zayd and 'Amr, by contrast, are both described as "human" (a species) based on their shared trait of being rational animals.

Differentia (*faṣl*) is an attribute that distinguishes one species of things from another. This thing that distinguishes it is said to be an essential quality or an essential "difference" that answers the question "which is it" rather than "what is it?" For instance, once we have further defined that Zayd is an animal (genus) and a human (species), we need another way to describe Zayd to distinguish him from 'Amr or 'Ā'isha. For example, if 'Amr and 'Ā'isha have different mothers, his distinguishing trait is that he is the son of Maryam. This makes "son of Maryam" a differentia in this case.

Aristotle objected to Plato's view that sensory knowledge was lesser in its reality and truth than types of knowledge that are derived through thought and philosophical understanding. Aristotle offered an alternative method of acquiring knowledge; namely, through demonstrative science, which held that information gathered from the sensory world is more true than theory and ideas that reside in the mind's perception.

Translation

[10] As for accidental [universals], their separation from the quiddity (*māhiya*) [of an entity] is inhibited and this is an **attached accident** (*ʿaraḍ lāzim*), or their separation is not inhibited and this is a **detached accident** (*ʿaraḍ al-mufāriq*). Each of these two [types of accidents] is specific to one true nature and this is the **property** (*khāṣṣa*). For example, [this could be] the capacity (*quwwa*) and act (*fiʿl*) of laughing in relation to a human. It [laughter] is described as a universal that can be attributed to those with a single true nature [i.e., humans] as an accidental trait.

[11] Or it [the accidental universal] can be attributed to more than one true nature [e.g., not exclusively to humans] and is therefore a **general accident** (*ʿaraḍ al-ʿāmm*). This is like breathing in [terms of] capacity (*quwwa*) and action (*fiʿl*) for humans and [for] others from [among] the animals. This [accidental universal] is described as a universal that can be applied to a variety of true natures (*ḥaqāʾiq*) as an accidental trait.

Explanatory Notes

As noted, an accident (*ʿaraḍ*) is a trait that is not essential to the object's identity (i.e., quiddity, *māhiya*). A trait is considered universal because it is a non-essential property that can be applied to a variety of objects, not only the specific object described. Accidents can be specific (*khāṣṣ*) to one group of many individuals that fit into this group, or accidents can be general (*ʿāmm*) and apply to individual entities in the group as well as others outside it. An accident that is specific to one group is known as a property (*khāṣṣa*) in the context of the five predicables (*kulliyāt al-khams*). Al-Abharī uses the term specific accident (*'araḍ khāṣṣa*) to convey this general idea.

A detached specific accident (*'araḍ khāṣṣ mufāriq*) is one that can be separated from the object described, as in al-Abharī's example of a laughing human. Laughter is universal to many humans and not just the specific person described, therefore it is a universal. It is specific enough that (according to this text), laughter can only be applied to humans and therefore it defines a particularity of the true nature (*ḥaqā'iq*) of humans while still being universal or common enough that it can potentially be applied to every human on the planet. Therefore, we can still say that laughter is a universal (*kullī*) trait. Laughter is also non-essential or non-conditional for a human to be human. Therefore, it is an accident (*'araḍ*).

The term *ḥaqīqa* ("true nature") refers to a group of the same things, a group whose "sameness" is based on the true nature of those entities. Thus, despite the many differences among humankind, humans still possess a true nature that places them in the category of humans. Al-Abharī is examining the accidents—both specific (*khāṣṣ*) and general (*'āmm*)—that apply to the true nature (*ḥaqīqa*) of humans.

Thus, accidents are further divided into general and specific. A general accident (*'araḍ 'āmm*), like breathing, is a property that Zayd shares with other non-humans, like horses and cats. Furthermore, breathing is considered an accidental (*'araḍī*) universal and not an essential (*dhātī*) property that defines Zayd's humanity because it is not an essential property that distinguishes Zayd or humans as human.

However, the capacity (*quwwa*) to breathe is necessary to Zayd's staying alive. This makes the *potentiality* to breathe an inseparable general accident (*'araḍ 'āmm lāzim*). However, in terms of action (*fi'l*), it is possible for Zayd to hold his breath for a while. Thus, the act of breathing is separate, making it a separate general accident (*'araḍ 'āmm mufāriq*).

By contrast, laughing is an accident in that it does not define one's humanity. Yet, it is still considered unique to humans. Therefore, laughter is a specific accident (*ʿaraḍ khāṣṣ*), that is, a non-essential property specific to humans. There is yet another dimension to this.

The act (*fiʿl*) of laughter is not necessary for an individual human like Zayd. It is only his capacity (*quwwa*) to laugh that is deemed necessary and thus the accident is attached (*lāzim*) to Zayd's identification as a human. That is, it is entirely possible for Zayd to be completely serious and never laugh in his entire life, despite his human capacity to laugh. This makes the *act* (*fiʿl*) of laughter a specific separable accident (*ʿaraḍ khāṣṣ mufāriq*). However, the accidental property related to laughter that is inseparable from Zayd is his capacity or potential (*quwwa*) to laugh. Thus, even though he may never actually laugh, one of his uniquely human traits is that he has the ability to laugh, unlike fish or cats who do not have the capacity to laugh and have not ever laughed in actuality. This makes the capacity (*quwwa*) to laugh a specific inseparable accident (*ʿaraḍ khāṣṣ lāzim*) while the act (*fiʿl*) of laughter remains a specific separable accident (*ʿaraḍ khāṣṣ mufāriq*).[8]

This is illustrated below.

Universals

1. **Essential (*dhātī*)**
    a. **Genus (*jins*)**: e.g., using "animal" to refer to humans
    b. **Species (*nawʿ*)**: e.g., humans
    c. **Differentia (*faṣl*)**: e.g., "rational" in reference to humans
2. Accidental
    a. **Property (*khāṣṣa*)**
        i. Separable (*mufāriq*): e.g., the act (*fiʿl*) of laughing with regard to humans

8 al-Maghnīsī, *Mughnī al-ṭullāb*, 114–119.

   ii. Inseparable (*lāzim*): e.g., the capacity (*quwwa*) to laugh with regard to humans

b. **General Accidents (*'araḍ 'āmm*)**

   i. Separable (*mufāriq*): e.g., the act (*fi'l*) of breathing with regard to humans

   ii. Inseparable (*lāzim*): e.g., the capacity (*quwwa*) to breathe with regard to humans

Translation

Expository Statement

[12] **Definition** (*ḥadd*): A statement that signifies the quiddity (*māhiya*) of a thing. It is composed of the close genus (*jins*) and close differentia (*faṣl,*) such as "rational animal" to [define] a human. This is also a **complete definition** (*ḥadd al-tāmm*).

[13] **Incomplete Definition** (*al-ḥadd al-nāqiṣ*): It is composed of a distant genus of a thing and a close differentia, such as "rational body" in reference to a human.

[14] **Complete Description** (*al-rasm al-tāmm*): It is composed of a close genus and a specific inseparable property (*khawāssihi al-lāzima*) such as "laughing animal" to define a human.

[15] **Incomplete Description** (*al-rasm al-nāqiṣ*): It is composed of accidents whose combinations are specific to one true nature. For example, describing a human by saying that he walks on two feet, [he has] wide nails, a hairless body, [he] stands upright, and laughs by nature.

Explanatory Notes

A definition that is complete describes exactly what an object is by using the closest genus possible and a specific difference, as a distinguishing feature to exclude the possibility of it being an alternative object. As mentioned in the text, a genus is described as a universal category that can be applied to a variety of entities that differ in their true nature (*mukhtalifīn bi-l-ḥaqā'iq*), in response to the question "what is it." A close genus means using a universal category that can be applied to a number of different types of objects and narrowing it down as much as possible without losing its universality. Thus, for example, rather than saying a created being (*makhlūq*), the genus is further narrowed to specify animal, because things like plants and rocks can also be considered in the category of "created beings."

The genus is then coupled with a specific difference that describes the object in a way that excludes everything other than the object described. Thus, to the genus of "animal" we would add the differentia (*faṣl*) of rationality. Among animals, humans are distinguished by their capacity to rationalize. Thus, al-Abharī provides the term "rational animal" (*ḥaywān nāṭiq*) as a complete definition in which the combination of these two words describe the object accurately and precisely.

An incomplete definition refers to a genus that is broader in its inclusion of the varieties of objects in it. So, for example, a "rational created being" (*makhlūq nāṭiq*) could still refer to humans, but since created beings can include a wider variety of objects such as plants and mountains, which go beyond the close genus of animal, its lack of precision causes it to be considered an incomplete definition (*ḥadd nāqiṣ*).

The next two ways of describing something is by description. A complete description is defined as being a combination of a close genus (as described in the previous discussion) and as an attached accident that is particular to an object's true nature; for example, using a laughing animal to describe humans. Animal is a close genus and laughter is a non-essential trait (therefore an accident) that is unique to humans; that is, laughter is a specific attached accident (*ʿaraḍ khāṣṣ lāzim*). Another example might be to say a "striped animal." This reference brings to mind a zebra. Yet it is possible for a zebra to be born without stripes and still be a zebra. Therefore, its stripes are non-essential to its "zebra-hood" (quiddity; *māhiya*). This means stripes are an attached non-essential trait of zebras.

Finally, a fourth way to refer to objects is with an incomplete description. In this case we do not use an essential property or genus to refer to the object. Instead, we use two or more accidents whose combination refers to the true nature of one particular object. For example, referring to a human by describing him as "he who walks on two feet, has a hairless body, stands upright, and laughs by nature." The combination of these accidents points to one possible object, namely humans. The combination of these accidents reflects one true nature (*ḥaqīqa wāḥida*), that of humans. The result is another way to refer to humans through a combination of accidents, although this is considered a less precise method and therefore an "incomplete" (*nāqiṣ*) description.

Translation

Propositions

[16] A proposition (*qaḍiyya*) is a statement about which it is valid to say to its claimant that he is truthful or untruthful [i.e., in his statement]. Additionally, it is either a categorical proposition (*ḥamliyya*), as in the phrase: "Zayd is a writer," or it is a conjunctive conditional proposition (*sharṭiyyatun muttaṣila*), as in the statement: "If the sun has risen, it is daytime." Or it is a disjunctive conditional proposition (*sharṭiyyatun munfaṣila*), as in the statement: "Numbers are either even or odd." The first part of the categorical proposition (*ḥamliyya*) is known as the subject term (*mawḍūʿ*) and the second [part] is the predicate term (*maḥmūl*). The first part of the conditional [proposition] is termed the antecedent (*muqaddam*) and the second part is the consequent (*tālī*).

Explanatory Notes

This section begins with what is known as a ***qaḍiyya*** or what logicians refer to as a **propositional statement.** To test whether or not a statement is a proposition, we check whether it can be true or false. Statements like the sky is red, this shirt is blue, and bears like honey are all statements that can be either true or false. Examples of statements that cannot be verified or falsified include questions like "How are you?," or imperative statements such as "Lock the door." Propositional statements take three forms which al-Abharī outlines.

The first is what is referred to in English logic texts as a "**categorical proposition,**" which al-Abharī refers to as *al-qaḍiyya al-ḥamliyya.* The term categorical proposition comes from the concept that each term used in language comes from what is known as a "categorical term." A categorical term is a noun or noun phrase. Zayd and writer are each categorical terms, when examined separately in and of themselves. A proposition links these two terms by claiming a factual relationship between them that can be true or false.

Furthermore, categorical terms in categorical propositions are divided into two further components.

One component is the subject term (*mawḍūʿ*) and the second component is the predicate term (*maḥmūl*). The term *maḥmūl* (from the root ḥ-m-l, "to carry") is preferred over the Arabic grammatical term for predicate (*khabar*) because of the concept of distribution. In a categorical proposition the predicate has information that is "carried over" or distributed to each of the members of the first categorical term, which is the subject. Thus, the predicate is *maḥmūl* ("carried"). In English we say it is "distributed." In the example above, *Zaydun kātibun* ("Zayd is a writer"), Zayd is the *mawḍūʿ* (subject), while writer (*kātibun*) is the predicate term (*maḥmūl*). The informative quality of the predicate term, writer (*kātibun*), is "carried over" by distributing information about Zayd.

One may ask, what happens if the propositional statement is a negation, such as, "Zayd is not a writer." In this case, Zayd may still be the subject, but since his status as a writer is denied, is writer still "carrying" a meaning that is being "distributed" to Zayd. Is writer still a *maḥmūl*? Based on commentators on the *Isagoge*, the answer to this question is that the predicate ("is not a writer") still carries or distributes a meaning which is in the negative. That is, "writer" is still considered a *maḥmūl* because it still gives information about Zayd, even if the information is a statement of negation of the predicate (*maḥmūl*). Negative statements are still referred to as composites of a subject (*mawḍūʿ*) and predicate (*maḥmūl*).

A **conjunctive conditional proposition** (***sharṭiyyatun muttaṣila***) means that in a statement, "if A then B," A and B must both be true in order for the statement to be true. In the example above, "if the sun is in the sky then it is daytime," both the antecedent (A) and the consequent (B) must be true at the same time. Thus the negation of A would also result in the negation of B. So, if the sun is not in the sky, then it is dark or it is not daytime. That is, in a conjunctive conditional proposition, both conjuncts must be true for the entire statement to be true.

A strong **disjunctive conditional proposition (*sharṭiyyatun munfaṣila*)** is a conditional statement in which only one of the two parts of the conditional proposition can be true, and both cannot be true at the same time. For example, a number cannot be both even and odd. It must be either even or odd.

Logicians make a distinction between strong disjunctive propositions in which only one of the parts of the "either/or" statement can be true, as in the conditional statements above, and weak disjunctive propositions that are non-conditional; in these it is possible for both parts of the statement to be true. For example, if we say, "the traveler would like to rest or eat," it is possible for the traveler to both rest and eat. This is categorized as a weak disjunctive proposition because the opposition between the two segments is not imperative.

Additionally, in grammar, conditional sentences are often divided into an "if clause" or condition for the first part and a second part, which is the "main clause" or the result. In logic, the former is referred to as the antecedent (*muqaddam*) and the latter is the consequent (*tālī*). For example, in the sentence "If the sun is out, then it is daytime," "If the sun is out" is the antecedent (*muqaddam*) and "then it is daytime" is the consequent (*tālī*).

Translation

[17] A categorical proposition is either affirmative (*mūjiba*) as in our statement, "Zayd is a writer," or it is negative (*sāliba*), as in our statement, "Zayd is not a writer." Additionally, each of these is either **singular** (*makhṣūṣa*) as we mentioned or a **quantified universal proposition** (*kulliyya musawwara*), as in our statement, "every human is a writer" and "no human is a writer." Or [each of these propositions is] a **quantified particular proposition** (*juz'iyya musawwara*), as in our statement, "some humans are writers" and "some humans are not writers." Or it can be unlike these, in which case it is referred to as indefinite (*muhmala*), as in our statement, "the human is a writer" and "the human is not a writer."

Explanatory Notes

The first section refers to what is known as the "quality" of propositions that either affirm or deny something. An affirmative (*mūjiba*) proposition affirms the connection or equivalence between the subject and the predicate of the categorical proposition. A categorical proposition that is negative (*sāliba*) denies the connection or equivalence of the subject and predicate. Al-Abharī states that categorical propositions must be either positive or negative. The two examples provided were "Zayd is a writer" and "Zayd is not a writer."

Each of these statements are then divided into the following three categories.

1) **Singular Categorical Propositions (*qaḍiyya makhṣūṣa*):** While al-Abharī uses the term *makhṣūṣa* to mean specified, the technical term used in English in the context of logic is "singular." This

means that the exact subject who is doing something is a specific or singular individual. In the example "Zayd is a writer," Zayd is the specific individual who is identified in this categorical proposition, thus "Zayd" gives it a precise meaning. This means that Zayd, and not Zaynab or Aḥmad or anyone else, is referred to as a writer.

2) **Quantified Universal Propositions (*kulliyatun musawwara*):** These are statements in which the subject is linked to a universal term that indicates "how much," or what logicians refer to as the "quantity" of something. Subjects of a proposition, such as "all people," or the use of what is known in Arabic grammar as the *lām al-istighrāq,* which is the use of "the" (that is, the indefinite article) to mean the generality of everything that falls under the word that follows "the" is in this category when it is clear that the word "the" (*al-*) is being used in this way. This clarification distinguishes it from indefinite propositions we see below.

In Arabic, the word *musawwara* literally means restricted. It may not seem that words like "all" and "every" are restrictive in meaning, but they are restrictive in the sense of "fencing in" or "surrounding" a subject with a universal term that quantifies it; hence they are *musawwara.* The root s-w-r means to surround or enclose something. This stands in contrast to *qaḍiyya muhmala* (indefinite propositions), as we see later. A more detailed discussion of quantifiers follows.

3) **Quantified Particular Propositions (*juz'iyya musawwara*):** These are categorical statements that partially quantify the subject with a term. For example, "*some* people" or "*one* person" do not specify who the person is; if this were specified, it would be a singular proposition (*makhṣūṣa*).

Translation

[18] Conjunctive [conditional propositions] are either **necessary** (*luzūmiyya*), as in our statement, "if the sun is out then it is daytime" or they are **contingent** (*ittifāqiyya*), as in our statement, "if humans are rational then donkeys bray." The disjunctive [conditional proposition] is either a strong [disjunctive], as in our statement, "numbers are either even or odd," and they (the disjuncts) are simultaneously **mutually exclusive and cannot be collectively false** (*māniʿat al-jamʿ wa-māniʿat al-khuluww*).

[19] Or they are only mutually exclusive, as in our statement, "this thing is either a rock or a tree."

[20] Or they can only be not collectively false, as in our statement, "Zayd is either in the water or he is not drowning."

[21] Disjunctive propositions can also be in three parts, as in our statement, "numbers are either greater [than], lesser [than], or equal [to]."

Explanatory Notes

A necessary (*luzūmiyya*) conjunctive conditional proposition means that if one part of the condition is true, then the other part must also, necessarily, be true. That is, in such a proposition if the antecedent is true, then the consequent is also necessarily true. Thus, in the example: "if the sun is out it is daytime," it is not possible for the sun to be out and for it not to be daytime. Logicians call this a "necessary" conjunctive conditional proposition.

In **contingent propositions**, the subject and predicate are attached to one another by concurrence or accident. This is known in Arabic texts of logic as *ittifāqiyya* which translates, literally, as "concurrence," though the technical equivalent in English logic is "contingent." This alludes to the idea that the truth of an antecedent does not necessitate the affirmation or denial of a consequent. The two may not be directly related or their concurrence may be a matter of coincidence rather than a linked cause.

Thus, in the example above, "if humans are rational then donkeys bray," it is true that humans are rational and it is true that donkeys bray. But humans are rational independently of whether or not donkeys bray. Similarly, donkeys bray whether humans are rational or not. The two conjuncts are linked without a necessary connection between them even though they are both true. The consequent (i.e., donkeys bray) is also contingent, in that this may be absent or present without affecting the truth of the antecedent (i.e., humans are rational).

A **disjunctive conditional proposition** is a statement in which one, some, or none of the disjuncts of the statement can be true. Thus, it is "disjunctive" (*munfaṣila*) as opposed to a conjunctive proposition in which both conjuncts are either true or false. The disjunctive conditional proposition is further divided into what is known in English logic as a strong disjunctive proposition (*ḥaqīqiyya*) and a weak disjunctive proposition. Strong propositions are both mutually exclusive (*māniʿat al-jamʿ*) and cannot be collectively false (*māniʿat al-khuluww*). Weak disjunctive propositions are mutually exclusive or disjuncts that cannot be collectively false but are not mutually exclusive.

The term mutually exclusive (*māniʿat al-jamʿ*) means that the two disjuncts in a disjunctive proposition cannot be true at the same time. The truth of one excludes the truth of the other. The term *māniʿat al-khuluww* means that the disjuncts cannot both be false—one has to be true. It is possible to have a weak disjunctive proposition in which the disjuncts cannot both be true and are therefore mutually exclusive, but they can both be false. In the example al-Abharī provides of such a weak disjunctive, that is, "the thing is either a rock or a tree," the rock and tree are mutually exclusive. One thing cannot be both a rock and a tree. However, the statement can be collectively false, in that the thing can be neither a rock nor a tree. Thus, this disjunctive proposition is not what is known as *māniʿat al-khuluww.*

Another example of a weak disjunct may be, "the traveler would like to keep driving or sleep." The two disjuncts are mutually exclusive, as the traveler cannot sleep and drive at the same time. However, the disjuncts can be collectively false. It is possible that the traveler does not want to drive or sleep, but would like to stop for dinner instead.

A weak disjunct could be one that is not mutually exclusive but is not collectively false. Al-Abharī gives the example, "Zayd is in the water, or he is not drowning." It is possible for both disjuncts to be true; Zayd can be in the water and also not be drowning. Therefore, the disjuncts are not mutually exclusive. However, both disjuncts cannot be false. The only way to drown is to be in the water. Therefore, saying that he is *not* "not drowning" means he is drowning and he cannot at the same time *not* be in the water.[9] Thus, this disjunctive proposition is collectively false (*māniʿat al-khuluww*) but not mutually exclusive (*māniʿat al-jamʿ*).

Note that some translate *māniʿat al-khuluww* as "collectively exhaustive." However, in this context, this is an error. The term "collectively exhaustive" requires that one option out of many must be absolutely true in the way that when rolling dice, the possibilities exhaust each other but one outcome must always be true. This case is not *māniʿat al-khuluww* since it is possible for more than one outcome to be true, unlike the example of dice, in which only one outcome can be true. It is possible for Zayd to be in the water and not drowning. The two disjuncts in the example al-Abharī provides do not collectively exhaust one another.

Finally, when al-Abharī states that a proposition can be in three parts or have three options (for example, Zayd can be studying, sleeping, or

9 That is, if he is drowning, he must be in the water.

eating) in a conditional statement, he means that disjunctive conditional propositions are not limited to statements based on paired disjuncts. How the various disjuncts can be true or false is beyond the scope of the examples provided in the *Isagoge*.

Translation

Opposition

[22] Opposition is a difference between two categorical propositions in [terms of] affirmation or negation such that one of them must be true and the other must be false, as in our statements, "Zayd is a writer" and "Zayd is not a writer." This is not established, except after[10] there is [a complete] equivalence of the subject, predicate, timing, place, relationship,[11] capacity and action,[12] universals and particulars, and conditions.[13]

---

10 That is, it can only be established after a complete equivalence is established.

11 *Iḍāfa* refers to the compound relationship of the subject such as, "brother-in-law" or "sister-in-law." Since these compound relationships are all ultimately subjects, the inclusion here may in fact be redundant; it serves to emphasize the author's point that everything must be an exact equivalent.

12 Capacity and action (*quwwa wa-l-fiʿl*) are philosophical concepts referring to someone's potential to do something versus their actually doing it. Actuality is a capacity that is acted out. For example, ʿĀ'isha is breathing in actuality and not breathing in potentiality. This is not contradictory because, for example, having the potential to not breath (i.e., by holding one's breath) does not necessarily mean that one is not breathing in actuality.

13 The conditions in propositions must agree. For example, one proposition states, "if it is 70 degrees ʿĀ'isha will be cold" and another proposition states, "if it is 75 degrees ʿĀ'isha will be hot"; the two propositions do not contradict each other because the conditions differ (in one, the condition states that it is 70 degrees and in the other, it is 75 degrees).

Explanatory Notes

Propositional statements make statements that affirm or deny certain claims based on the relationship between the subject and the predicate of the proposition. This means that the affirmation or negation in one form of a categorical proposition will lead to a relationship with another proposition that conveys the opposite meaning. In logic, these related propositions that convey opposing meanings are known as **oppositions**. Each structure of each categorical proposition requires that its opposing proposition be formed in a particular correlating structure in order to retain its truth value.

Al-Abharī begins his discussion of oppositions with the most simple form, which is known as a **singular proposition.** This refers to a specified object or individual as the subject of the categorical proposition. In such a statement, it is sufficient to simply contradict the singular proposition to convey its opposite meaning. Al-Abharī provides the proposition "Zayd is a writer." This is a singular proposition, in that the subject, "Zayd," refers to a specific individual. Specific individuals are also spoken of as universals or "wholes." That is, when we say Zayd is a writer, it is understood that all of Zayd is a writer and not one-quarter of Zayd or some part of Zayd.

Therefore, the contradictory oppositional proposition is simply formed with a negation. This process is also true for propositions that make statements about existence, such as "'Ā'isha exists." For this rule to be applicable the two singular statements (that is, the proposition and opposition) must be exactly the same in subject and predicate. They must not have any *temporal qualifiers* that change the nature of the subject or predicate in the oppositional proposition. Al-Abharī gives a list of temporal qualifiers such as time, location, relationship, etc. that can alter the equivalence of the subject and predicate in another categorical proposition; this, in turn, means that the contradiction is not an oppositional proposition in relation to the original.

Below are examples that further elucidate the temporal qualifiers that al-Abharī mentions in his text of the *Isagoge*.

Difference in subject: Zaynab is sitting ≠ ʿUmar is not sitting.

Difference in the predicate: Zaynab is standing ≠ Zaynab is not eating.

Difference in timing: Zaynab was fasting yesterday ≠ Zaynab is not fasting today.

Difference in location: Zaynab is not productive at home ≠ Zaynab is productive at work.

Difference in relationship (*iḍāfa*): Zaynab is Aḥmad's aunt ≠ Zaynab is not ʿĀ'isha's aunt.

Difference in potentiality and actuality: Zaynab is, in potentiality, a good writer ≠ Zaynab is not, in actuality, a good writer.

Difference in universals and particulars: Zaynab is white [her skin tone as a whole] ≠ Zaynab is dark [in part, when referring to her eyes].

Difference in conditions: Zaynab likes to work [when she is at her job] ≠ Zaynab does not like to work [when she is on vacation].

Note that the rules for deriving oppositional statements rest on what is known as the **principle of non-contradiction.** This states that it is impossible for two contradictory statements to both be true and it is impossible for them to both be false. However, in order for this principle of non-contradiction to be applicable to two statements, they must be exactly the same in every way, including all of the temporal qualifiers al-Abharī lists in the examples above. Otherwise, because a qualifier may alter the subject or predicate of the original categorical proposition, two statements that may appear contradictory may not be truly contradictory.

If we return to al-Abharī's example, "Zayd is a writer," the only way to contradict this type of singular statement is by saying the exact same thing with the exact same qualities (i.e., time, place, etc.) and by stating contradictory things about them (i.e., in the case above,

"Zayd is not a writer"). For example, the statement "Zayd is writing in the morning" and "Zayd is not writing in the afternoon," is not a contradictory opposition because the temporal quality differs. Similarly, a true contradiction involves referring to the exact same subject and the same thing attributed to the subject, then affirming it in one proposition and negating it in another. Commentaries on the *Isagoge* by some later scholars have simplified the above by stating that the entirety of the subject and predicate must be exactly the same.

Translation

[23] The [contradictory] opposition of a **universal affirmative proposition** is a **particular negative proposition.** And the [contradictory] opposition of a **universal negative proposition is a particular affirmative proposition**, such as our statement: "all humans are animals" and "some humans are not animals." As well as [our statements]: "no human is an animal" and "some humans are animals."

[24] **Two quantified propositions** (*maḥṣūratān*) do not establish a [contradictory] opposition between them except by differing in the [quantity of their] universals and particulars. This is because two universal propositions can both be false, such as our statements, "all humans are writers" and "no humans are writers." [Similarly], two particular propositions can both be true, as in our statements, "some humans are writers" and "some humans are not writers."

Explanatory Notes

Qualities and Quantities of Propositions

Propositions are said to have both qualities and quantities. **Qualities** either affirm or deny relationships between subjects and predicates in a proposition. Thus, when we say "'Ā'isha is a scholar," the quality of this proposition is an affirmation that binds the subject and the predicate. Similarly, if we say "'Ā'isha is not a scholar" we have established a quality of denial in this proposition in which the subject and the predicate have a relationship of difference.

Quantities of propositions involve the question, "how much?" In the context of non-singular (that is, universal and particular) categorical propositions, the quantity of a proposition specifies the extent of the subject, for example, all, some, every. Thus, every subject of a proposition is either singular, universal, or particular based on what is known as its quantity. Universal propositions are universal if the subject is referred to its entirety rather than its parts. Words such as, "every" and "all" and negative terms such as "no," and "none" are universals. Particulars refer to the restricted extent of a subject. Quantifiers such "some" and "many" are examples of terms that precede a subject and make the proposition particular, based on the particularity of its subject.

Universal and Particular Quantifiers

Below are some of the most common examples of quantifiers used to denote universal and particular statements.

Universal Quantifiers

All—All humans are rational

Any—Any human is rational

None—None of the humans are rational

No one—No one is rational

No—No human is rational

Never—Humans are never rational

S/he who—She who is human is rational

One who—One who is human is rational

Whatever—Whatever is human is rational

Whoever—Whoever is human is rational

Particular Quantifiers

Some—Some humans are rational

Often—Often humans are rational

Several—Several humans are rational

Commonly—Commonly, humans are rational

Most—Most humans are rational

Usually—Usually humans are rational

Sometimes—Sometimes humans are rational

Frequently—Frequently humans are rational

In the Western scholastic discourse on logic, the variations of quantities and qualities of categorical propositions have been labeled based on the Latin words *affirmo* (I affirm) and *nego* (I deny). The two propositions with affirmative qualities (A and I) were derived from the first two vowels in the word AffIrmo. The two negative propositions (E and O) were derived from the two vowels in the words nEgO. Thus, in English logic texts the following abbreviations are used for the variations of categorical propositions that relate to quality and quantity.

A: Universal Affirmative Proposition

E: Universal Negative Proposition

I: Particular Affirmative Proposition

O: Particular Negative Proposition

Each proposition (A, E, I, and O) has a different form of opposition that can be formed with the other. The forms of opposition are contradictory, contrary, and subcontrary opposition. To define these terms, we utilize a well-known logic diagram known as the **square of opposition.**

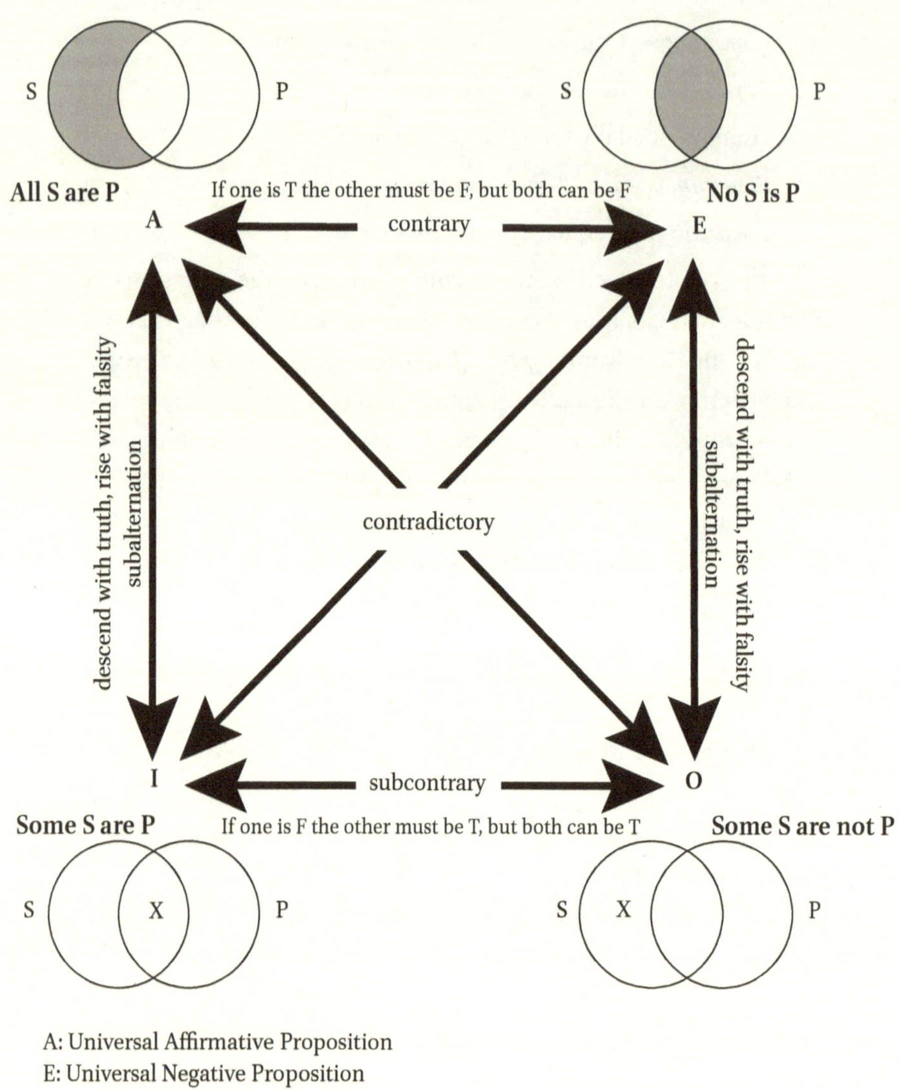

A: Universal Affirmative Proposition
E: Universal Negative Proposition
I: Particular Affirmative Proposition
O: Particular Negative Proposition
Minor Term (S) = Subject
Major Term (P) = Predicate

Diagram 2: Square of opposition

Contradictory, Contrary, Subcontrary, and Subalternative Oppositions

Contradictory oppositions are those in which two categorical propositions necessitate that one is true and the other is false. This means that the two statements are true contradictions that follow the principle of non-contradiction, which holds that both statements cannot be true and false at the same time. The denial of one categorical proposition by its contradictory opposition is a denial of both quantity and quality.

Thus, based upon the diagram 2 above, "A" and "O" are contradictory oppositions and "E" and "I" are contradictory oppositions. Al-Abharī says this in the *Isagoge* when he writes that the opposition of a universal affirmative proposition is a particular negative proposition. A universal affirmative proposition is an A proposition. A particular negative proposition is an O proposition. The square of opposition (see diagram 2) confirms this statement by illustrating that an A proposition is contradicted by an O oppositional proposition and vice versa.

Similarly, al-Abharī writes that the opposition of a universal negative proposition (that is, an E proposition) is a particular affirmative proposition (that is, an I proposition). The square of opposition (diagram 2) illustrates the same principle highlighted by al-Abharī; that is, the contradictory opposition of an E proposition is an I proposition and vice versa.

The examples of contradictory oppositions al-Abharī provides are the A proposition "all humans are animals" and the O proposition "some humans are not animals." If we use the universal phrase *all* to claim that humans are animals, then the existence of even one example to the contrary is sufficient to contradict this statement. Thus, the statement "*some* humans are not animals" means that the claim that humans are *all* animals is altogether false.

Additionally, al-Abharī uses the E proposition, "no human is an animal," to establish a contradictory opposition with the I proposition, "some humans are animals." Using the same logic as above, it is clear why one statement must be true and the other must be false. In these two cases, they cannot both be true or both be false. Note that in the *Isagoge* al-Abharī is referring to a *contradictory opposition.* He discusses contrary and subcontrary oppositions below.

Contrary oppositions are those in which both oppositions cannot be true but they can both be false. This type of opposition occurs between A and E propositions, as is evident in the square of opposition (diagram 2). Both A and E oppositions are forms of universal oppositions that include exhaustive or extreme statements in the affirmative or negative. As a result, it is possible that particular propositions do not include the extremes in A and E that can be true while both the A and E universal statements are false. Contradictory and contrary oppositions differ in that in **contradictory** oppositions one proposition must be true while the other is false (that is, they cannot both be false), while in **contrary** oppositions both propositions can be false.

Al-Abharī refers to this possibility of both statements being false when he states: Two quantified propositions (*maḥṣūratān*) are not opposed unless they differ in the quality of their universals and particulars because two universal propositions can both be false, as in our statements, "all humans are writers" and "no humans are writers."

As mentioned above, two universals cannot establish a contradictory opposition, they can only establish a contrary opposition that means that they can both be false. "All humans are writers" and "no humans are writers" are examples of two universal statements (that is, with the same quantity) that differ in quality. While it is possible for one to be true and the other false, there is a third possibility in which al-Abharī's first proposition is not true, nor is the second. Thus, they are contrary but not contradictory oppositions.

Subcontrary oppositions are those in which both propositions cannot be false but both can be true. This type of opposition occurs between the particular I and O statements that are illustrated in the bottom of the square of opposition (diagram 2). Since particular statements refer to specific segments, it is possible for two statements to refer to differing parts of the whole; therefore, both can be true. However, since an affirmative particular statement implies that there is a negative particular statement that is also true (otherwise it would have been a universal statement), two similar particular statements with different qualities cannot both be false.

When al-Abharī says that two particular propositions can both be true, as in our statements, "some humans are writers" and "some humans are not writers," this is what he means. That is, some humans can be writers and some humans cannot be writers are equally true statements. If Zaynab is a writer, it is possible for ʿĀ'isha to not be a writer. However, they cannot both be false because our usage of the particular term "*some* humans are writers" means that there are also *some* who are not (otherwise, we would have said "*all* humans are writers").

Subalternative oppositions are two similar propositions that differ in quantity but agree in quality. This is not mentioned by al-Abharī in his *Isagoge* but we introduce this concept for future reference and further clarification in understanding the square of opposition (diagram 2). In the square of opposition, subalternation occurs between the two vertical points of the square. That is, subalternation occurs between A and I propositions on the left side of the square and E and O propositions on the right side of the square.

The two top points of the square refer to universals. They subalternate with particulars of the same quality directly below them. This means that since the particular is part of the universal whole, when the universal is true, the particular is also true. Based on the square, if the top two universals (A in relation to I or E in relation to O) are true, then the corresponding bottom propositions I and O are also true. However, the opposite is not the case. If the bottom two are false, then the top two are also false. But if the bottom two (I in relation to A and O in relation to E) are true, the top two corresponding universals (A and E) are not necessarily also true.

In the context of the square this relationship is known as "descending with truth and rising with falsity." That is, the truth of the top universals descends to the bottom particulars, making them both true. And the falsity of the two bottom particulars rises to make the corresponding universals at the top of the square true. Venn diagrams can be used to illustrate the same relationship in another format.

Translation

Conversion

[25] Conversion (*'aks al-mustawī*) [involves] the subject term being made into the predicate term and the predicate term being made into the subject term while maintaining the affirmative or negative [quality of the proposition], and [maintaining its] truth or falsehood. A universal affirmative proposition does not convert to a universal proposition. Although our statement, "every human is an animal" is true, the converse that "every animal is a human" is not true. Therefore, it [i.e., the statement "every animal is a human"] must convert to a particular proposition. This is [true] because if we say, "every human is an animal," it would be accurate [to say], "some animals are humans." [This is true because] we find elements of specific traits in [both] humans and animals. Thus, it is [true] that "some animals are humans."

[26] Based on this reasoning, a particular affirmative proposition is also converted as a particular proposition. A universal negative proposition is converted as a universal proposition. This is self-evident, because if it is true that, "no stone is a human," then it is [also] true that, "no human is a stone." A particular negative proposition has no necessary conversion [pattern] because our statement, "some animals are not humans," is true, whereas its conversion is not true.

Explanatory Notes

Conversion (*'aks al-mustawī*) is a process in which the subject and the predicate are reversed while maintaining the the propositions' affirmative or negative quality and its truth value. That is, rather than stating the opposite of a proposition (the way we did in earlier oppositional statements), in a conversion, we state the same thing in a different way. For a conversion to do this, there are rules to follow based on the quantity and quality of each proposition. The new proposition that results after a subject and predicate are switched is known as the converse. According to the rules for proper conversion, there are two types of conversion, a simple conversion and conversion by limitation.

Simple Conversion and Conversion by Limitation

Simple conversion is a process by which the subject and the predicate are switched without making any other changes to its quality or quantity. This is valid only for universal negative propositions (E propositions) and particular affirmative propositions (I propositions). When al-Abharī writes, "A particular affirmative proposition is also converted as a particular proposition based on this reasoning," he is referring to I propositions. This means that the I proposition, "some S is P," can be converted by simple conversion to, "some P is S."

Al-Abharī also gives an example of E propositions in the section on conversion when he writes: "A universal negative proposition is converted as a universal proposition. And this is clearly self-evident, because if it is true that, 'no stone is a human,' then it is [also] true that, 'no human is a stone.'"

This type of conversion process is known as a "simple conversion" because, as we see in the example, the subject and predicate *simply* switch, while maintaining the truth value of the statement.

Conversion by limitation entails two steps. The first step involves switching the subject and the predicate. The second step involves adjusting the quantity. This process is used to convert universal affirmative (A) propositions. This is indicated in al-Abharī's statement, "a universal affirmative proposition does not convert to a universal proposition." The process for conversion by limitation for A propositions involves adjusting the quantity from universal to particular. Thus, if it is said 'every S is P,' the converse would be 'some P is S.'"

The example al-Abharī provides is the universal A proposition, "every human is an animal." The reversal of the subject and predicate without adjusting its quality would be invalid in terms of its truth value because, as al-Abharī states, "we find elements of specific traits in [both] humans and animals." He means that the category of animal is broader than the category of human. This relates to the concept of **distribution** in logic. When a term applies to the entirety of another term, we say it is distributed. Universal propositions always distribute the predicate to the entirety of the subject, but this is not the case when they are reversed. That is, "all animals" distributes itself to "all humans," meaning that there is no human that is not an animal. However, the category of animal is broader than the category of human because it includes other non-human animals. This means a subject of a broader category cannot be used universally as a predicate of a narrower category because the predicate in this case would **not be distributed** to the subject. Thus, universal propositions must be made into particular propositions as a part of their conversion process. This is what al-Abharī means when he says:

> "Every human is an animal" is true, the converse that "every animal is a human" is not true. Therefore, it must convert as a particular proposition. This is because if we said, "every human is an animal," it would be accurate [to say], "some animals are humans."

O propositions or particular negative propositions do not have any set rule by which they can be converted. The simple conversion rules and the conversion by limitation rules only apply to A, I, and E propositions. This is what al-Abharī means in his statement: "A particular negative proposition has no necessary conversion [pattern]. This is because our statement, 'some animals are not humans,' is true, whereas its conversion is not true."

Obversion (*'aks al-naqīḍ*)

Finally, note that obversion is another form by which we can make the same statement in terms of truth value while adjusting the quality of the proposition. An obversion involves denying the contradictory opposition of a proposition to affirm the same truth of a proposition. An obversion is based on the premise that if a proposition is true, then a denial of its contradiction will retain the same truth. Obversion is known in Arabic as *'aks al-naqīḍ*, as opposed to conversion, which is known as *'aks al-mustawī*. Although al-Abharī does not discuss obversion, later commentaries on the *Isagoge* and other logic texts mention it. We also find these concepts in the study of debate and disputation (*'ilm al-baḥth wa-l-munāẓara*). The following are examples of obversion.

Zaynab is a distinguished writer.

Obversion: *Zaynab is not an undistinguished writer.*

'Umar always runs fast

Obversion: *'Umar does not ever not run fast.*

The process of proper obversion entails two steps. *First*, the quality of the proposition must change. *Second*, the predicate must be negated.

Step One: "Humans are rational," changes to "humans are irrational."

Step Two: "Humans are irrational" changes to "humans are not irrational."

Thus, the obversion of the statement, "humans are rational," is "humans are not irrational."

Translation

The Syllogism

[27] [A syllogism] is an assertion[14] composed of [other] assertions, which if accepted as true, necessitates another assertion. It can be a **correlative [syllogism]** (*iqtirānī*), such as our statement: "each body is formed," and "each thing which is formed is temporal" therefore "each body is temporal." Alternatively, it can be a **selective [syllogism]** (*istithnā'ī*), such as our statement, "if the sun is out, then it is daytime." However, "it is not daytime," therefore, "the sun is not out."

Explanatory Notes

Inductive and Deductive Reasoning

When we form inferences or conclusions in our minds about matters that we do not already have information about, then we must use one of two methods of reasoning. The first method of reasoning is **inductive reasoning** and the second is **deductive reasoning**. In both cases, we use pre-established concepts, that is, propositions that are taken to be truths to establish a relationship between these assertions and derive another assertion known as the conclusion. In Arabic logic, this relationship between assertions that establishes a conclusion by necessity (i.e., *luzūmiyya*) is known as *nisba*.

Inductive reasoning relies on the observation of consistent recurrences of certain matters from which we can derive a conclusion based

14 Other editions add the phrase, *malfūẓun aw maʿqūlun* ("either articulated or conceptualized").

on the assumption that the recurrence will continue. This type of conclusion may be derived from scientific experimentation or the way we form common beliefs about how the world operates. Examples of inductive reasoning include the following.

Alexander the Great was mortal.

Muhammad Ali was mortal.

Malcolm X was mortal.

Everyone who lived in the eighteenth century was mortal.

Therefore, I must also be mortal.

This conclusion is reached through inductive reasoning, after seeing a prevalent pattern (in this case death), it can be assumed to apply to other similar instances (in this case all humans in the eighteenth century). Inductive reasoning is foundational to deriving conclusions from scientific laboratory work, in which scientists conduct extensive experiments with controls, to look for consistent patterns and gather knowledge about how microorganisms or chemicals operate.

The second way to derive conclusions is through the use of deductive reasoning. **Deductive reasoning involves combining a number of pre-established concepts (*taṣawwurāt*) that have a common link in order to derive new conclusions based on the evidence of the connections between these concepts.** The study of logic focuses on the study of deductive reasoning.

The Syllogism (*qiyās*) and Its Forms: Correlative (*iqtirānī*) and Selective (*istithnāʾī*) Syllogisms

The word *qiyās* ("syllogism") comes from a root word that means "to measure," "to judge," "to correlate," and/or "to draw comparisons." This implies that when we engage in *qiyās*, we are weighing one thing against another. In the context of logical arguments, we are comparing two or more statements that are connected to one another. When one statement is considered true, its relationship with another connected statement results in a new statement or conclusion based on this connection.

Al-Abharī notes that syllogisms have two forms, syllogisms of correlation (*iqtirānī*) and selective syllogisms (*istithnā'ī*). The most common example used to demonstrate the combined syllogism is S=M, M=P, therefore S=P. In the correlative syllogism the key identifying factor is the importance of the premises; the entirety of the conclusion (S=P) cannot be reached without the premises leading up to it. Thus, two propositions are combined to result in the conclusion, since only parts of the conclusion are in each of the premises.

This combination of two propositions in a syllogism occurs by way of a connecting term that recurs in both propositions, which in turn connects the two premises by way of "mediation." This connection between the two propositions is called "correlation" (*muqārana*); it necessitates a new statement in the form of a conclusion. Thus, **syllogisms that are derived from correlating propositions that contain a mediating phrase or term that connects them are known in Arabic logic as *qiyās al-iqtirānī* (syllogisms of correlation).** The following sections of the *Isagoge* detail about the ways in which these types of syllogisms are established.

A selective syllogism (*qiyās al-isthithnā'ī*) is a syllogism in which the conclusion or the opposite of the conclusion appears in one of the two propositions leading to the conclusion. Since it appears *in its full form* in one of the propositions, a selective syllogism is said to appear in actuality (*bi-l-fi'l*), This stands in contrast to syllogisms of correlation, in which the entirety of the conclusion does not appear in the premises, but rather results from the implied connection between the premises. In the case of syllogisms of correlation, this "appearance" of a conclusion through implication is said to be an appearance in potentiality (*bi-l-quwwa*).

In a selective syllogism, the major premise (which is the first premise in the syllogism) also contains a conditional "if-then" statement. The example al-Abharī provides of conditional syllogisms is, "if the sun has risen, then it is daylight." The conditional premise that contains the "if-statement" is known as *muqaddima sharṭiyya.* The minor premise (which is the second premise in the syllogism, that is, the "then-statement") is a categorical proposition (*qaḍiyya ḥamliyya*) in which the predicate or subject of the first premise is affirmed or denied. In this case, we might say that one of the conditions is "selected" in the selective syllogisms. If the second premise affirms the first premise, it is known as an affirmative premise (*wāḍiʿa*). If the minor premise negates the first premise it is known as negational premise (*rāfiʿa*).

The following is an example of an **affirmative selective syllogism.**

> If the sun has risen, it is daytime. [Premise 1]
>
> The sun has risen. [Premise 2]
>
> Therefore, it is daytime. [Consequent]

The following is an example of a **negative selective syllogism.**

> If the sun has risen, it is daytime. [Premise 1]
>
> It is not daytime. [Premise 2]
>
> Therefore, the sun has not risen. [Consequent]

Note that in both cases the consequent or its contradiction is expressed explicitly (*bi-l-fiʿl*) in the first premise ("the sun has risen") of the selective syllogism. Furthermore, in a conditional syllogism: "If A, then B," the conditional element "If A" is known as the antecedent (*muqaddam*). The result "then B" is known as the consequent (*tālī*).

There are two additional rules related to conditional syllogisms:

1. ***An affirmation of the antecedent must result in an affirmation of the consequent. But an affirmation of the consequent does not necessitate an affirmation of the antecedent.*** For example, in the conditional proposition, "if Zaynab is a human [being], she is a living being," affirming Zaynab's humanity necessitates affirming her status as a living being. In fact, an affirmation that she is a living being does not

necessarily mean she is a human being. She could be a cat, a plant, or a goat.

2. ***A negation of the consequent necessitates a negation of the antecedent, but a negation of the antecedent does not necessitate a negation of the consequent.*** In the example, "if Zaynab is a human [being], she is a living being," if we say Zaynab is not a living being, we would have to conclude that she is not a human [being], but if we say she is not a human being, she could still be another type of living being.

Translation

[28] What is repeated between the two premises of the syllogism is referred to as the "**middle term**" (*ḥadd awsaṭ*). The subject of the conclusion is referred to as the minor term (*ḥadd aṣghar*) and its predicate is the **major term** (*ḥadd akbar*). The premise that contains the **minor term** is referred to as the **minor** [premise] (*ṣughrā*) and the one that contains the major term is known as the **major** [premise] (*kubrā*). The structural composition of the major and minor premises [of the syllogism] is called a figure (*shakl*).

Explanatory Notes

As mentioned, a syllogism is a combination of propositions that necessarily lead to a third proposition that takes the form of a conclusion. Thus, the basic structure of a syllogism is made up of three propositions. Propositions 1 and 2 function as what are known as premises, while proposition 3 functions as the conclusion. The premises are the supporting evidence that lead to a particular conclusion, that a particular subject (S) equals a particular predicate (P) or what is often symbolized as S=P. The subject of the conclusion (S) is known as the minor term (*ḥadd aṣghar*). The predicate (P) of the conclusion is known as the major term (*ḥadd akbar*).

The two premises that lead to the conclusion are connected by what is known as a middle term. The middle term creates the correlation between the two propositions and makes them function as premises (by creating new information in the form of a third proposition, known as the conclusion). This connector or link between the two premises of the syllogism is known as the "**middle term**" (*ḥadd awsaṭ*), and is often represented as "M" in logical formulas.

Syllogisms are always made of three propositions. The premise that contains the subject of the conclusion is known as the **minor premise**. The premise that contains the predicate of the conclusion is known as the **major premise**. The predicate and the premise containing the predicate are characterized as "major" because the predicate of a conclusion is ideally more general and more universal than the subject. The subject and the premise containing the subject are referred to as "minor" because, ideally, the subject is more specific or particular than the predicate.

The equation of the subject (the minor premise) and the predicate (the major premise) is known as the conclusion. In the conclusion, the middle term is always eliminated although it appears in both the minor and major premise. The structure of the syllogism, in terms of the placement of the middle term in the premises, is known as the figure (*shakl*) of the syllogism. Below is an example of the structure of a syllogism.

M=P — Major Premise (*Kubrā*)

S=M — Minor Premise (*Ṣughrā*)

S=P — Conclusion

The middle term is M *because* it is repeated in both premises. The minor term is S because it is the subject (*mawḍūʿ*) of the conclusion (S=P). The major term is P because it is the predicate (*maḥmūl*) of the conclusion (S=P). The minor premise is S=M because it includes the minor term (S). The major premise is M=P because it includes the major term (P).

Translation

[29] There are four figures [of syllogisms]. If the middle term is the predicate in the minor premise and the subject in the major premise, then it is the **first figure**. If it is the inversion [of this] then it is the **fourth figure**. If [the middle term] is the subject in both [premises] then it is the **third figure**. If [the middle term] is the predicate in both [premises], then it is the **second figure**. These are the four figures outlined in logic.

Explanatory Notes

Al-Abharī recognizes four figures of syllogisms; these figures are defined by the placement of the middle term in the minor and major premises, as elucidated below.

Figure 1

M=P [Major Premise]

S=M [Minor Premise]

S=P [Conclusion]

In figure 1, the middle term M is the subject in the major premise (M=P) and it is the predicate in the minor premise (S=M). An example of this follows:

Every human (M) is rational (P) [**Major Premise**]

Zayd (S) is a human (M) [**Minor Premise**]

Therefore, Zayd (S) is rational (P) [**Conclusion**]

Figure 2

P=M [Major Premise]

S=M [Minor Premise]

S=P [Conclusion]

In figure 2, the middle term (M) is the predicate in both premises.

Figure 3

M=P [Major Premise]

M=S [Minor Premise]

S=P [Conclusion]

In figure 3, the middle term is the subject in both premises.

Figure 4

P=M [Major Premise]

M=S [Minor Premise]

S=P [Conclusion]

In figure 4, the middle term is the subject in the minor premise and the predicate in the major premise. That is, as al-Abharī states, it is an inversion of the first figure.

Translation

[30] The fourth figure is exceedingly distant from what is natural. One with a sound mind and a steady disposition does not need to revert the second [figure] into the first [figure]. The second [figure] is derived when there is a contradiction between the two premises [by way of] either affirmation or negation. The first figure is the one that has been considered the standard for [deductive] knowledge. We presented it here to form a blueprint and derive what is requested.

Explanatory Notes

Validity vs. Truth of Syllogisms

As mentioned, a correlative syllogism is formed when two premises have a common connection in the form of their middle term. When this middle term forms a connection between two premises, then the conclusion is inferred by necessity. If the premises are assumed to be true and the connecting middle term has a valid connection between the two premises, then the conclusion is both valid and true. However, if the premises are not true but the syllogistic process by which the two premises are connected through the middle term is sound, then the syllogism is valid but the truth of the conclusion may or may not be true. In such a case, it is said that the truth of the conclusion is undetermined. On the other hand, if both the premises are true and the conclusion is false, then there must be a fallacy in the syllogistic reasoning that makes the syllogism itself invalid.

The following is an example of a syllogism that is valid but untrue:

Unicorns always have a single horn

Adam is a unicorn

Therefore, Adam has a single horn

The connection between the two premises above is valid. Therefore, the syllogism is valid. But the conclusion and all of the premises are clearly false, since unicorns do not exist. Therefore, it is important to distinguish between a valid conclusion based on valid syllogistic reasoning and a true conclusion. More details about what makes syllogisms valid follow; for now, I examine the kinds of valid syllogisms al-Abharī describes in this section.

The following is an example of an invalid syllogism with a true conclusion.

All humans are rational beings

Adam is a human

Therefore, all humans are mortal

The premises above are all true and the conclusion is also a true statement. However, the syllogism is invalid because the connection between the premises and the conclusion is insufficient. A valid syllogism can only have three terms: A major, minor, and middle term. The conclusion has a fourth term, "mortal," which makes the syllogism invalid. A syllogism that is invalid because of an extra term is known as a **fourth term fallacy**. Thus, we can see that premises and conclusions in a syllogism can be true statements but the validity of the syllogistic process itself is a separate matter.

Some Forms of Valid Syllogisms Presented by al-Abharī

After presenting the four figures (*shakl*) of a syllogism and understanding the placement of the middle term, al-Abharī explains that he included the fourth figure for the sake of thoroughness, but in practice the fourth figure is rarely, if ever, used to make an argument. He states that the fourth figure mentioned, in which the middle term is the subject in the minor premise and a predicate in the major premise, is a convoluted form of making an argument and is not commonly used because of its lack of clarity. Al-Abharī also explains that the second figure is not as clear as the first figure but it is still understandable to someone with a strong rational ability.

He also explains that figure 2 has two conditions that must be fulfilled in order to reach a valid conclusion. First, if one of the premises is affirmative, the other must be negative. Second, one of the two premises must be a universal proposition. The conclusion of the second form is always a particular negative proposition or a universal negative proposition. That is, the conclusion is always a negative statement.

Figures 3 and 4 are always a particular affirmative or a particular negative conclusion. That is, the conclusion of figures 3 and 4 must always be particular. Figure 4 must fulfill a number of other conditions in order to result in a valid conclusion. If the major premise is universal, one of the two premises must be affirmative and the other premise negative. If the minor premise is universal, both the premises must be affirmative.

As al-Abharī states, the most ideal and clear form of the syllogism is that of figure 1. Logicians refer to figure 1 as the "perfect syllogism." This is because in making a strong argument, one aims to use figure 1 syllogisms, since the other figures do not always yield clear results. This is why when attempting to make a clear argument, there is an effort to transform figures 2–4 into the first figure when possible. For instance, one can transform figure 2 into figure 1, by changing the major premise into its converse (*ʿaks al-mustawī*) to render it into a figure 1 syllogism.

Translation

[There are] four optimal moods

[31] **First:** As in our statement, "each body is formed" and "each thing that has been formed is temporal," therefore, "each body is temporal."

[32] **Second:** As in our statement, "each body is formed," and "nothing that is formed is eternal," therefore "no body is eternal."

[33] **Third:** As in our statement, "some bodies are formed," and "everything that is formed is temporal," therefore "some bodies are temporal."

[34] **Fourth:** As in our statement, "some bodies are formed," and "nothing that is formed is eternal," therefore, "some bodies are not eternal."

Explanatory Notes

Forms, Figures, and Moods of Syllogisms

The term "mood" comes from the Latin term *modus*, which means "way." Aristotle used this Latin term, from the Greek term *tropos*, in his *Prior Analytics* to discuss the different types of premise combinations for the figures listed previously that result in valid conclusions. In Arabic the term is *ḍarb* (pl. *ḍurūb*). **Each figure has a set of moods that are combinations of premises that differ in terms of the quality and quantity, such as AAA or EAE.** However, not all of these combinations yield valid conclusions.

The form of a syllogism is the combination of a syllogism's figure, which describes the position of the middle term in the premises, and the mood of each of these premises. If we multiply the possible moods with the possible figures, we would find a total of 256 possible syllogistic forms. The vast majority of these forms, however, do not yield valid conclusions and thus are ignored in the study of logic. In order to list valid forms of syllogisms, we must review our abbreviations for the quality and quantity of syllogisms below.

A: Universal Affirmative Proposition

E: Universal Negative Proposition

I: Particular Affirmative Proposition

O: Particular Negative Proposition

Al-Abharī demonstrates the four valid forms of a figure 1 syllogism, probably to keep his *Isagoge* a simple text for the beginner. Remember that a figure 1 syllogism is

M=P [Major Premise]

S=M [Minor Premise]

Therefore, S=P [Conclusion]

Another way to illustrate the valid moods for figure 1 syllogisms follows.

Valid Forms of Syllogisms for Figure 1

	BARBARA		**CELARENT**
A	Every M is P	E	No M is P
A	Every S is M	A	Every S is M
A	Therefore, every S is P	E	Therefore, no S is P
	DARII		**FERIO**
A	Every M is P	E	No M is P
I	Some S is M	I	Some S is M
I	Therefore, some S is P	O	Therefore, some S is not P

Al-Abharī's *Isagoge* outlines the four valid forms of figure 1 syllogisms highlighted in the illustration above, with one significant difference. Al-Abharī lists the the minor premise before the major premise when outlining the structure of the four figures. This means that it may appear, initially, that the English syllogistic forms in the chart above do not correspond to what al-Abharī lists. That is, what is an AII syllogism in English appears to be an IAI syllogism in Arabic. This brings us to an important principle.

With regard to mood, it is important to highlight a significant difference in the way English and Arabic logic is often written. In English logic texts, syllogisms are written in a format in which the major premise precedes the minor premise, which, in turn, is used to derive the mood of the syllogism. In al-Abharī's text and other Arabic logic texts that read from right to left, the minor (*ṣughrā*) premise is mentioned before the major (*kubrā*) premise. Thus, if we want to translate this from Arabic into moods represented in the Latin alphabet, we must invert the major premise and the minor premise, so that the major premise is first and the minor premise is listed second. This enables us to correlate the standard symbols for moods for each figure used in European-based logic texts to those in Arabic logic texts. We can see how this applies to the examples al-Abharī gives in the *Isagoge*.

The first statement that al-Abharī mentions is one in which the minor premise is universal affirmative (A) and the major premise is universal affirmative (A). The conclusion is universal affirmative (A). The mood of this syllogism is AAA. This is demonstrated below. Since they are all As, there is no need to invert the order of the minor and major premise here.

> Each body is formed [**universal affirmative minor premise A**]
>
> Each thing that is formed is temporal [**universal affirmative major premise A**]
>
> Therefore, each body is temporal [**universal affirmative conclusion A**]

In the second statement, al-Abharī mentions a minor premise (universal affirmative (A)) and a major premise (universal negative (E)). The conclusion is therefore a universal negative (E). The mood of this syllogism as presented in this Arabic text appears to be AEE. However, A and E must be inverted for it to translate into the moods used in figure 1 in standard English logic texts. In English, after inverting these, the mood is EAE, as below.

> Each body is formed [universal affirmative minor premise A]
>
> Nothing that is formed is eternal [universal negative major premise E]
>
> Therefore, no body is eternal [universal negative conclusion E]

In the third statement in al-Abharī's text, the minor premise is particular affirmative (I) and the major premise is universal affirmative (A). The conclusion is a particular affirmative (I) statement. In Arabic the mood of the syllogism is IAI. When we invert the minor and major premises it becomes AII in English logic, as below.

> Some bodies are formed [particular affirmative minor premise I]
>
> Nothing that is formed is eternal [universal affirmative major premise A]
>
> Therefore, some bodies are temporal [particular affirmative conclusion I]

In the fourth statement in al-Abharī's text, the minor premise is particular affirmative (I) and the major premise is universal negative (E). The conclusion is a particular negative (O) statement. In Arabic the mood for this syllogism is IEO. When we invert the minor and major premises it becomes EIO in English logic.

> Some bodies are formed [particular affirmative minor premise I]
>
> Nothing that is formed is eternal [universal negative major premise E]
>
> Some bodies are not eternal [particular negative conclusion O]

We can illustrate the other figures in a chart similar to that of figure 1.

Valid Syllogism Forms for Figure 2

	CESARE		CAMESTRES
E	No P is M	A	Every P is M
A	Every S is M	E	No S is M
E	Therefore, no S is P	E	Therefore, no S is P
	FESTINO		**BAROCO**
E	No P is M	A	Every P is M
I	Some S is M	O	Some S is not M
O	Therefore, some S is not P	O	Therefore, some S is not P

Valid Syllogism Forms for Figure 3

	DARAPTI		DISAMIS
A	Every M is P	I	Some M is P
A	Every M is S	A	Every M is S
I	Therefore, some S is P	I	Therefore, some S is P
	DATISI		**FELAPTON**
A	Every M is P	E	No M is P
I	Some M is S	A	Every M is S
I	Therefore, some S is P	O	Therefore, some S is not P
	BOCARDO		**FERISON**
O	Some M is not P	E	No M is P
A	Every M is S	I	Some M is S
O	Therefore, some S is not P	O	Therefore, some S is not P

Meanings Represented in the Names of Syllogistic Figures

Each of the forms of valid syllogisms above have been named using a mnemonic list that is often memorized. Figure 1 syllogisms are Barbara,

Celarent, Darii, and Ferio. Figure 2 syllogisms are Cesare, Camastres, Festino, and Baroco. Figure 3 syllogisms are Darapti, Disamis, Datisi, Felapton, Bocardo, and Ferison.

First: The names for each of these syllogisms include valuable information about the syllogism they refer to. As noted, the first figure is the most perfect syllogism. This means that figure 2 and figure 3 syllogisms can be reduced to figure 1 syllogisms to form more perfect arguments. The first letter of each of the figure 2 and 3 syllogisms represents the first letter of the figure 1 syllogism they can be reduced to. For example, Felapton can be reduced to Ferio. Baroco can be reduced to Barbara and Camestres can be reduced to Celarent.

Second: Each vowel in each name represents the mood of the syllogism it refers to. So BArbArA is a AAA syllogism. CElArEnt is an EAE syllogism. DArAptI is an AAI syllogism. This logic applies to all of the names of the syllogisms.

Third: The consonants that follow each vowel represent the reduction method of each proposition represented by each vowel. Below is a list of what the consonants represent.

> **S:** simple conversion
>
> **P:** conversion by limitation
>
> **M:** transposition
>
> **C:** reduction by contradiction

Consonants in the name that are not S, P, M, or C indicate that the proposition in the vowel preceding this consonant cannot be reduced. Reduction is explained in greater detail below.

Reduction of Figure 2 and Figure 3 Syllogisms

Figure 2 syllogisms are regarded as useful in debates, to refute the arguments of adversaries because they always result in negative conclusions. Figure 3 syllogisms are useful for challenging assumptions about the universality of a premise because they always result in particular statements that point to contradictory exceptions to universalisms.

Generally, however, scholars of logic attempt to reduce figure 2 and 3 syllogisms to figure 1 syllogisms in order to produce tighter and clearer arguments.

We mentioned four ways to reduce propositions in figure 2 and 3 syllogisms to figure 1 syllogisms. Each of these are explained in detail below.

S: Simple Conversion occurs when a vowel is followed by an S. A simple conversion occurs by switching the predicate and the subject of a proposition. This only works for E and I propositions. So, "no S is M" can be converted to "no M is S" or "some S is M" can be converted to "some M is S."

P: Conversion by limitation is only applied to A propositions. Conversion by limitation involves switching the subject and the predicate of the proposition and then making the universal A statement into a particular statement. Thus, "every S is P" becomes "some P is S."

M: Transposition is the process by which the major and minor premises are transposed. The major premise becomes the minor premise and the minor premise becomes the major premise.

C: Reduction by contradiction is only used to reduce Bocardo and Baroco syllogisms to a Barbara syllogism. Reducing a Bocardo or Baroco syllogism is difficult because they are composed of A and O premises. Converting the A premise leaves two particular premises that violate the rules of a valid syllogism. In this case, if an opponent has accepted the premises of an argument as true, we show that its conclusion must also be true by proving that its negation would create a contradiction in the premises an opponent has already accepted.

The process of doing this involves converting the conclusion to its contradiction, then replacing the new contradictory conclusion with the O premise in the syllogism. This results in a Barbara syllogism with a new conclusion that contradicts one of the original premises. The goal is to demonstrate that if one accepts the premises in the prior argument, but not its conclusion, one contradicts oneself. This contradiction then indirectly proves that the original conclusion had to be true.

Example

Every human is rational

Some plants are not rational

Therefore, some plants are not humans

We begin by changing the conclusion of the original, "therefore, some plants are not humans," to its contradictory converse, "every plant is a human." The next step is to replace the new conclusion with the O premise in the original syllogism. The new syllogism is the following:

Every human is rational

Every plant is human

Therefore, every plant is rational

This new form is reached through reduction by contradiction. Also note that the Baroco syllogism is now a Barbara syllogism. Here we have demonstrated that a contradiction of the conclusion of the original creates a new syllogism that contradicts the premises of the original that were already accepted. In the new syllogism, "every plant is rational" contradicts the premise in the original syllogism, "some plants are not rational." In demonstrating this contradiction that occurs if one does not accept the conclusion of the original, we have indirectly supported the conclusion of the Baroco syllogism in the form of its corresponding Barbara syllogism. This is reduction by contradiction. The following example is a reduction by contradiction for a Bocardo syllogism.

Some humans do not laugh

Every being with feet is human

Therefore, some beings with feet do not laugh

Again, we change the conclusion, "some beings with feet do not laugh," to its contrary "every being with feet laughs," then we replace this with the O premise in the original syllogism.

Every being with feet laughs

Every being with feet is human

Therefore, every human laughs

The new conclusion contradicts the major premise of the original. Thus, through this indirect method, we can use the contradiction that is established in the new Barbara syllogism after its reduction from the Bocardo syllogism to find another way to say that the conclusion of the Bocardo syllogism must be accepted because its contrary cannot be true while the premises of the original are true. This is a complicated way of saying one must accept the Bocardo syllogism by highlighting the contradictions that occur if one accepts the contradictory converse of the Bocardo syllogism's conclusion that leads to the Barbara syllogism.

This is confusing at first. The process of reduction through contradiction only applies to two syllogistic forms, Baroco in figure 2 and Bocardo in figure 3. Fortunately, understanding syllogisms and their reductions does not hinge on how well one understands this complex process.

The following is an example of a simpler reduction. Below is an example of a Cesare syllogism.

No human is a plant

Every cactus is a plant

No cactus is human

The middle term, "plant" is in the position for figure 2 syllogisms. We also see that this is an EAE syllogism known by the form Cesare when this mood appears in figure 2. The C in Cesare indicates that its reduction would be another C syllogism in figure 1, namely Celarent. The "s" after the "e" in Cesare indicates that we must do a simple conversion for the E syllogism in the premise of Cesare. Since none of the other consonants in the word Cesare represents any reduction symbols, we do not have to do anything with the other propositions in this syllogism. Thus, the reduction of the Cesare syllogism to a Celarent syllogism is the following:

No plant is human

Every cactus is a plant

Therefore, no cactus is human

Below is an example of the reduction of a Darapti syllogism:

Every theologian likes al-Taftazānī

Every theologian reads Arabic

Therefore, some people who read Arabic like al-Taftazānī

The D in the Darapti syllogism indicates that we need to change this into a figure 1 Darii syllogism to reduce it. The "p" in Darapti tells us that we must do a conversion by limitation to the minor premise of this AAI syllogism. Thus, "every theologian reads Arabic," is changed to "some people who read Arabic are theologians." Thus the new Darii or AII figure 1 syllogism is as follows.

Every theologian likes al-Taftazānī

Some people who read Arabic are theologians (*conversion by limitation*)

Therefore, some people who read Arabic like al-Taftāzānī

Finally, we offer an example of transposition to reduce a Camestres syllogism.

Every ophthalmologist has a medical degree

No history professor has a medical degree

Therefore, no history professor is an ophthalmologist

The C in Camestres indicates that we must reduce this syllogism into Celarent. The "m" after the first "a" in Camestres indicates that the first A proposition in the syllogism (i.e., the major premise) must be transposed. The final "s" (after the two "es") indicates that the minor premise and conclusion must undergo a simple conversion. Thus the new syllogism becomes the following.

No one with a medical degree is a history professor (*simple conversion*)

Every ophthalmologist has a medical degree (*transposition*)

Therefore, no ophthalmologist is a history professor (*simple conversion*)

Below are illustrations of how figure 2 and figure 3 syllogisms can be reduced to figure 1 syllogisms.

Figure 2 Reductions

Figure 2	Reduction Method	Figure 1
Cesare		**Celarent**
No P is M	*Simple Conversion* →	No M is P
All S is M		All S is M
No S is P		No S is P
Camestres		**Celarent**
All P is M	*Simple Conversion* →	No M is S
No S is M	*Transposition* →	All P is M
No S is P	*Simple Conversion* →	No P is S
Festino		**Ferio**
No P is M	*Simple Conversion* →	No M is P
Some S is M		Some S is M
Some S is not P		Some S is not P
Baroco		**Barbara**
Every P is M	*Contradiction*	All P is M
Some S is not M	→	All S is P
Some S is not P	*Contradiction*	All S is M

Figure 3 Reductions

Figure 3	Reduction Method	Figure 1
Darapti		**Darii**
All M is P		All M is P
All M is S	*Conversion by Limitation* →	Some S is M
Some S is P		Some S is P
Disamis		**Darii**
Some M is P	*Transposition* →	All M is S
All M is S	*Simple Conversion* →	Some P is M
Some S is P	*Simple Conversion* →	Some P is S
Datisi		**Darii**
All M is P		All M is P
Some M is S	*Simple Conversion* →	Some S is M
Some S is P		Some S is P
Felapton		**Ferio**
No M is P		No M is P
All M is S	*Conversion by Limitation* →	Some S is M
Some S is not P		Some S is not P
Ferison		**Ferio**
No M is P		No M is P
Some M is S	*Simple Conversion* →	Some S is M
Some S is not P		Some S is not P
Bocardo		**Barbara**
Some M is not P	*Contradiction* →	All S is P
All M is S		All M is S
Some S is not P	*Contradiction*	All M is P

Translation

[35] **Correlative syllogisms** (*iqtirānī*) are composed of two categorical propositions, as encountered.

[36] Or they are composed of two conjunctive [propositions], as in our statement, "if the sun is out then it is daytime," and "every time it is daytime, the earth is illuminated," therefore, "if the sun is out, the earth is illuminated."

[37] Alternatively, a [correlative syllogism] can be composed of two disjunctive [propositions], as in our statement, "every [whole] number is either even or odd," and "every even number is either the pair of a pair or a pair of an odd number," therefore, "every number is either odd or a pair of a pair or the pair of an odd number."

[38] It can also be composed of a categorical (*ḥamliyya*) [proposition] and a conjunctive proposition, as in our statement, "as long as this [being] is human then he is [also] an animal," and "every animal is a body," therefore, "every being that is human is also a body."

[39] Or it can be composed of a categorical [proposition] and a disjunctive proposition, as in our statement, "each number is either even or odd," and "each even [number] can then be divided into two equals," therefore, "each number is either odd, or can be divided into two equals."

[40] Or it is composed of a conjunctive [proposition] and disjunctive [proposition], as in our statement, "as long as this [being] is human then he is an animal," and "every animal is either white or black," therefore, "as long as this [being] is human then he is either white or black."

Explanatory Notes

As mentioned, Muslim logicians divided syllogisms into those in which the conclusion is *potentially* present in one of the premises and those in which the conclusion was *actually* present. The former is defined as a correlative syllogism (*iqtirānī*) and the latter is defined as a selective syllogism (*istihnā'ī*). Al-Abharī states that the term "correlative" (*iqtirānī*) is used for these types of syllogisms because they are composed of separate propositions that have a parallel or correlative relationship that leads to a conclusion. The term *iqtirān* comes from the root q-r-n that means correlation, parallelism, and a simultaneous relationship (e.g., a *qarīna* refers to a close companion that often accompanies someone).

Correlative Syllogism

The correlative (*iqtirānī*) syllogism can be contrasted to the selective (*istithnā'ī*) syllogism in which the premises of the propositions are oppositional rather than correlative and one of the opposing segments of the premises must be selected to reach a conclusion. Hence, we prefer to translate this as a "selective" syllogism, because it best conveys its functional meaning. We discuss this further below.

Al-Abharī states that the correlative (*iqtirānī*) syllogism can be composed of two categorical propositions in the form of a major and a minor premise that results in a conclusion through the presence of a middle term (as we have seen). This simple syllogistic form is known as a categorical syllogism. Al-Abharī, however, does not divide syllogisms into categorical and compound, as texts on English logic do, rather he refers to correlative and selective syllogisms, as mentioned.

Correlative syllogisms can be composed of categorical propositions or they can be made up of compound propositions that correlate to lead to a conclusion. Al-Abharī lists possible combinations of categorical propositions, conjunctive compound propositions, and disjunctive compound propositions that can form premises that lead to a conclusion by correlation rather than through the opposition of the premises. In structures that include compound propositions, the middle term in the premises can take the form of a phrase or categorical statement that leads to a correlation between the two premises. Below are the examples of correlative syllogisms al-Abharī lists in the *Isagoge.*

1. Two conjunctive conditional propositions

If the sun is out then it is daytime.

Every time it is daytime, the earth is illuminated.

Therefore, "if the sun is out, the earth is illuminated."

The middle term here is "every time it is daytime." This middle term, which is common to both the major and minor premises, creates a correlation between the two conjunctive conditional propositions that leads to a correlation between them. This combination of these connected propositions are known as premises that lead to a conclusion. Together, the premises and conclusion are known as a syllogism. In this case, since a relationship of correlation rather than opposition has been formed between the premises, this syllogism is known as a correlative (*iqtirānī*) syllogism.

Al-Abharī did not distinguish between the conjunctive proposition and the conditional proposition in the *Isagoge*. It appears that he considered both to be forms of conjunctive propositions. This is unlike the divisions of syllogisms in Western logic, in which conditional propositions and conjunctive propositions are separate subgroups of compound propositions.

2. Two disjunctive propositions

Every [whole] number is either even or odd.

Every even number is either the pair of a pair[15] or a pair of an odd number.[16]

Therefore, every number is either odd or a pair of a pair or the pair of an odd number.

In this example two disjunctive propositions correlate with one another. The middle term is the phrase "every even number." This creates the connection between the two premises that leads to a conclusion.

3. Categorical proposition and conjunctive conditional proposition

As long as this [being] is human then he is [also] an animal.

Every animal is a body.

Therefore, every being which is human is also a body.

In this example, a conjunctive conditional proposition is structured as "if a then b." The conditional statement is, "as long as this being is human then he is [also] an animal." The second premise is a categorical proposition in which the subject is "every animal" and the predicate is "a body." The middle term in this syllogism is "animal." This middle term creates a correlative connection between the two premises that leads to a conclusion.

4. Categorical propositions and disjunctive propositions

Each number is either even or odd.

Each even [number] can then be divided into two equals.

Therefore, each number is either odd, or can be divided into two equals.

In this example, the first premise is a disjunctive proposition in the form of either "a" or "b." The second premise is a categorical proposition;

15 For example, "four is a pair of twos."

16 For example, "two is a pair of ones."

that is, even numbers are the subject and their ability to be divided into equal parts is the predicate. The middle term that forms a connection between the two premises is the "even number." The mutual connection between the two premises formed by the middle term "even numbers" leads to a relationship of correlation between these two premises, which in turn leads to a conclusion that produces new information. Thus, the example above is another form that a correlative syllogism can take based on the combination of a categorical proposition and disjunctive proposition connected by a middle term.

5. Conjunctive conditional propositions and disjunctive propositions

As long as this [being] is human then he is an animal.

Every animal is either white or black.

Therefore, as long as this [being] is human then he is either white or black.

The first premise is a conjunctive proposition because it is a conditional proposition in the form of "if a then b." The first premise states that "if he is human then he is an animal." The second premise is a disjunctive proposition because it is in the form of "either a or b" ("every animal is either black or white"). The middle term that connects the two premises is "every animal." This connection leads to a correlation that is found in the conclusion.

Translation

[41] As for the **selective syllogism**, (*al-qiyās al-istithnāʾī*) the conditional [proposition] is the major premise in it. If [the conditional syllogism] is **conjunctive**, then the [affirmative] selection of the antecedent results in the [affirmation of the] consequent itself. [This is according to] our saying, "if this is human then he is an animal. He is human. Therefore, he is an animal." And the selection of a negation of the consequent results in the negation of the antecedent. [This is according to] our saying, "if this is human then he is an animal. He is not an animal. Therefore, he is not human."

[42] If it is a strong (*ḥaqīqiyya*) **disjunctive syllogism**, the [affirmative] selection of one of the opposing two disjuncts results in the negation of the other and the selection of the negation of one [of the two opposing disjuncts] results in the affirmation of the other.

Explanatory Notes

How to Translate *istithnāʾī*

The translation of the term *istithnāʾī* has long been a dilemma for scholars of Arabic logic who write in English. Some have used a literal translation of the word and refer to this as a syllogism of "exclusion" or "exception."[17] This translation is problematic because it does not necessarily reflect the way al-Abharī uses it in his text, not to mention

17 Edwin Calverley, "al-Abharī's *Īsāghūjī fī 'l-Manṭiq*," in *The Macdonald Presentation Volume* (London: Oxford University Press, 1933).

other Arabic texts of logic and philosophy. Additionally, the use of the term *istithnāʾī* in Arabic logic differs from the way it is used in the field of Arabic grammar, where the word does indeed mean exception. It appears that some translators may have assumed that the meanings of this word are the same, without noting the distinctions between its use in the field of logic versus that of grammar.

Kwame Gyekye explores the technical meaning of the word *istithnāʾ* in the context of Arabic logic by examining the way Greek philosophical terms were translated into Arabic in early texts.[18] Gyekye states that in his translation of Aristotle's *Die Interpretation*, Isḥāq b. Ḥunayn translated the Greek word *prostithēmi* (prosthesis), which means "to add," as *istithnāʾ*.[19] Gyekye notes that *istithnāʾ* is also translated as *iḍāfa* and *zāda* in other places. Based on this, he argues that in its earliest appearance in texts of Arabic logic, the term *istithnāʾ* was used to mean "addition" and in this context, "additional assumption."

Gyekye argues that the concept of an "additional assumption" referred to as *proslēpsis* was used by the Stoics to refer to the minor premise of a conditional syllogism. *Proslēpsis* is a synonym for *prostithēmi* and both refer to a form of addition. The idea being that in a selective syllogism, the minor premise is an "additional assumption" that leads to a consequent.

Gyekye also notes that the word *istithnāʾ* is used in other texts as a translation of the term *prosdiorismos*, which means "further condition."[20] In combining these findings with other usages of the term *istithnāʾ* in Arabic texts, as well as Hebrew translations of texts of Arabic logic, he convincingly argues that the root of this word was most likely th-n-y, meaning "to duplicate" rather than that "to exclude."[21] The implied meaning is that the minor premise "duplicates" a portion of

18 Kwame Gyekye, "The Term Istithnā' in Arabic Logic," *Journal of the American Oriental Society* 92, no. 1 (Jan.–Mar. 1972): 88–92.

19 Gyekye, 88.

20 Gyekye, 89.

21 Gyekye, 91.

what appears in the major premise. He also writes that many Muslim philosophers who use the term *istithnā'* take the word for granted and do not explain its meaning or connection to the form of syllogisms they are referring to. Therefore, it is possible that originally, an early translation of the word from Greek may have been intended to mean "duplicate" or "add," but over time it came to be accepted as a term in the field of logic. The linguistic origins of the term *istithnā'* was later problematized by modern translators who attempted to capture the English equivalent of the term.[22]

Some commentators on the *Isagoge* argue that the term *istihnā'* means to exclude because the minor premise of a selective syllogism is introduced by the term *lākin* ("but"). This reasoning does not appear to be strong, however, in light of Gyekye's research into the origins of this term in Arabic texts of logic. It is also not necessary for the minor premise to begin with the term *lākin* in order for it to fit the criteria of the *istithnā'ī* syllogism as described by Ibn Sīnā's logic tradition and by extension by al-Abharī in his *Isagoge*.

Additionally, translating this term as "syllogisms of exception and exclusion," and "reduplicative propositions" is also inaccurate in relation to this portion of the text, as it does not correspond to these categories of syllogisms. **Exclusive syllogisms** are compound syllogisms in which two parts of the syllogism are joined with terms such as "only" or "alone." For example, "Zayd will only pass the exam if he studies. Zayd has studied. Therefore, he will pass the exam." **Syllogisms of exception** include terms such as "except" and "save." Everyone who takes the exam will fail, except those who study. Zayd has studied. Therefore, he will pass the exam." A **reduplicative syllogism** distributes a predicate to a subject with specific conditions. It uses phrases such as "as long as" and "as far as." For example, "Zayd, as a student, is successful." Therefore, there are duplicate statements being made about Zayd, in what appears to be one statement: "Zayd, as a student, is successful." Both duplicate

22 This understanding is also in line with that of the Stanford Philosophy. See https://plato.stanford.edu/entries/ibn-sina-logic/

statements embedded here must be true for the entire reduplicative statement to be true.

If we accept Gyekye's argument that the origins of *istithnāʾī* come from "duplicate," then it is the conclusion that is duplicated (i.e., that appears twice). It appears once in one of the premises and then reappears in the conclusion. This takes us back to our earlier discussion, based on commentators of the *Isagoge*, that in *istithnāʾī* syllogisms the conclusion appears explicitly (*bi-l-fiʿl*) and appears somewhere in the minor and major premises before the consequent. Thus, the consequent is "duplicated" in the sense that it appears in the premises as well as the consequent. As discussed, in correlative syllogisms (*iqtirānī*), the conclusion does not appear explicitly in the premises, rather it appears implicitly (*bi-l-quwwa*) by virtue of its correlative relationship formed by the middle term. This is a different form of duplication than the two true statements implied in a reduplicative syllogism. The use of "duplicate," "exception," and "exclusion" in the titles of different forms of these syllogisms above makes it easy to form a false equivalence to the *qiyās al-istithnāʾī* which functions differently from all three of these forms of syllogisms.

Functionally, rather than the premises having a correlative relationship as in correlative syllogisms, we see that a selection of part of the major premise leads to the consequent of an *istithnāʾī* syllogism. The term "selection," rather than "exclusion" or "exception," is a more accurate description of the internal syllogistic process that distinguishes the *istihnāʾī* syllogism.

For this reason, I have chosen to use "selective syllogism" as a translation for *qiyās al-istithnāʾī*, which stands opposite the correlative syllogism (*qiyās al-iqtirānī*). Al-Abharī also uses the term *istithnāʾ* to mean selection when he writes, if we "select" or affirm the antecedent then we also affirm the consequent in a conjunctive conditional proposition. It appears that despite its likely origins from the Greek term "duplicate," it has evolved contextually as "selection" in logic texts.

The Structural Variations of Selective Syllogisms

1. Conditional Conjunctive

Al-Abharī provides the basic structures of selective syllogisms in his *Isagoge*. The first is composed of a major premise (*mawḍūʿ*), in this case known as an antecedent (*muqaddam*), since it is a conditional proposition. The minor premise is a categorical proposition that either posits (*waḍʿ*) one of the terms of the condition in the major premise or negates one of the terms of the condition of the major premise.

Al-Abharī's use of the term *mawḍūʿ* might be confusing because, when the term is used in the context of the entire syllogism, the major premise is the proposition, that is, the *mawḍūʿ*. By contrast, when *mawḍūʿ* is used in the context of a categorical proposition (*ḥamliyya*), it is the subject (*mawḍūʿ*) and the predicate is known as *khabar*. The conclusion of a selective syllogism is known as the consequent (*tālī*). Al-Abharī provides the following example:

> If this is human then he is an animal. [**Major Premise/Antecedent**]
>
> He is human. [**Minor Premise**]
>
> Therefore, he is an animal. [**Consequent**]

Unlike the correlative syllogisms, the minor premise does not form a correlative relationship between the two premises through a middle term. Rather, in a selective syllogism, the minor premise forces a selection of one of the conditions set in the major premise. In this case, we must select either an affirmation or a negation of the major term. Also, the consequent is duplicated in the selective syllogism where "he is an animal" is mentioned explicitly (*bi-l-fiʿl*) in the premises, then appears again in the consequent.

In the *Isagoge* al-Abharī outlines the two forms of valid conditional syllogisms. The first form is with an antecedent that makes a conditional statement in the form of a major premise. This is followed by a minor premise that affirms the antecedent. In Western logic, this format is known as a method of affirming (Latin, *modus ponens*).

The second valid way to construct a conditional syllogism is by positing a conditional proposition in the antecedent, then denying the consequent. If the consequent is denied then the antecedent must also be denied. In Western logic, this is known as a method of denying (Latin, *modus tollens*). In both cases there is a parallel relationship similar to the rules of conditional propositions in which affirming the antecedent results in affirming the consequent. Similarly, denying the consequent results in denying the antecedent. This parallelism is what is referred to as a *luzūmiyya* ("necessary") parallel connection between the terms of the condition in the antecedent. In debates, making an argument by denying the consequent is useful if one is trying to demonstrate the absurdity of the antecedent. This method of argumentation is known as ***reductio ad absurdum***.

In addition, the affirmative and negative relationship between the antecedent and the consequent is not bidirectional. Since the consequent is universal or broader than the antecedent, an affirmation of the antecedent requires an affirmation of the consequent. But an affirmation of the consequent does not require an affirmation of the antecedent. Assuming the truth of the antecedent based on the truth of the consequent is known as **the fallacy of affirming the consequent.** The following example clarifies this:

If 'Ā'isha is studying, then she is at home.

'Ā'isha is studying.

Therefore, she is at home.

While the conditional statement in the major premise claims that 'Ā'isha must be at home if she is studying, it does not state that she must necessarily be studying if she is at home. The conditional statement is not bidirectional. 'Ā'isha can be at home doing something else, unrelated to studying. Thus, assuming that an affirmation of the consequent, "she is at home," necessitates an affirmation of the antecedent is an invalid conclusion and falls into the fallacy of affirming the consequent. However, the syllogism above, in which the antecedent is affirmed by stating that 'Ā'isha is studying is valid because affirming the antecedent results in affirming the consequent which is that she is at home.

In the *Isagoge* al-Abharī states that a negation of the consequent must result in the negation of the antecedent (i.e., *modus tollens*). But this rule too, is unidirectional. A negation of the antecedent does not require a negation of the consequent. For example,

If ʿĀ'isha is studying, then she is at home.

ʿĀ'isha is not studying.

Therefore, she is not at home.

Thus, this is an invalid syllogism because ʿĀ'isha can be at home, but not studying. But according to the major premise, if she is studying she *must* be at home. However, her being at home does not mean she is studying. Assuming that a negation of the antecedent requires a negation of the consequent is another fallacy known as the **fallacy of denying the antecedent**. It is helpful to recall the two major rules discussed earlier regarding the validity of conditional syllogisms. These are

1. If the antecedent is true, the consequent must also be true. However, this is unidirectional. The truth of the consequent does not require that the antecedent also be true.
2. To negate the consequent means that the antecedent must also be negated. But to negate the antecedent does not necessarily mean the consequent must also be negated.

2. Conjunctive Syllogisms

Although al-Abharī does not mention this explicitly in the *Isagoge*, it is helpful to also consider non-conditional conjunctive syllogisms, or what is known in English logic as "conjunctive syllogisms." **Conjunctive syllogisms are those that have a conjunctive proposition in the major premise that states that two conjuncts cannot occur simultaneously.** Rather than a format of "if A then B" that is characteristic of conjunctive conditional propositions, conjunctive syllogisms deny that two things can be joined without placing a conditional phrase in the major premise. The minor premise then affirms or negates one of the conjuncts. For example,

> No one can text and drive carefully at the same time.
>
> Zaynab is driving carefully.
>
> Therefore, she cannot be texting.

In the syllogism above two conjuncts are mutually exclusive, without being a conditional sentence. Furthermore, the minor premise is a selection of one of the conjuncts that leads to the consequent, thus making it a selective syllogism. However, for conjunctive syllogisms, certain rules for validity must be taken into account. First, we must consider the nature of the conjunctive proposition in the major premise. Are the two conjuncts exhaustive of any other possibilities not mentioned as conjuncts? If they are exhaustive of any other possibility other than the two conjuncts then we can either deny or affirm a conjunct in the major premise and the syllogism remains valid. For example:

> Zayd is either asleep or awake.
>
> Zayd is not asleep.
>
> Therefore, he must be awake.

This is a valid syllogism because the conjuncts are exhaustive of any possibility other than being asleep or awake. There are no third options. This means that it is valid for the minor premise to be a negation of one of the conjuncts. However, in a conjunctive syllogism that is not exhaustive of all other possibilities other than the conjuncts, a minor premise may affirm but cannot deny a conjunct to form a valid conclusion. The following is an example of such a conjunctive syllogism:

> Zayd is either asleep or baking a cake.
>
> Zayd is not asleep.
>
> Therefore, Zayd is baking a cake.

The above is an invalid syllogism because it is possible that Zayd is not asleep but that he is also not baking a cake. The two conjuncts are not exhaustive of the possibilities other than what is mentioned. Therefore, a denial in the minor premise is not valid, but an affirmation is valid. For example,

Zayd is either asleep or baking a cake.

Zayd is baking a cake.

Therefore, Zayd is not asleep.

Or

Zayd is either asleep or baking a cake.

Zayd is asleep.

Therefore, Zayd is not baking a cake.

In both cases the affirmation in the minor premise leads to a valid syllogism. Thus, the rule for conjunctive syllogisms is the following. If the conjuncts in the major premise are exhaustive of any possibility other than the conjuncts, then the minor premise can either affirm or negate the major premise. If the conjunctive proposition in the major premise is not exhaustive, then the minor premise can only affirm a conjunct in the major premise.

3. Disjunctive Syllogisms

Disjunctive syllogisms are the second form of selective syllogisms that al-Abharī highlights. Recall that disjunctive propositions are types of propositions that are "either-or" statements. In a disjunctive syllogism, a major premise is composed of a disjunctive proposition and the minor premise affirms or negates one of the disjuncts in the major premise, which is a disjunctive proposition. In doing so the minor premise selects one of the disjuncts, either a or b, by saying which one (a or b) it is. Al-Abharī simplifies his discussion of disjunctive syllogisms by focusing on strong disjunctive syllogisms, without mentioning weak disjunctive syllogisms. He uses the term *ḥaqīqī* (real) to refer to what is known in English logic as "strong" disjunctives.

From our discussion on strong and weak disjunctive propositions, we know that strong disjunctives are propositions in which only one of the disjuncts can be true. It is not possible for both of them to be true, as this makes them mutually exclusive (*māniʿat al-jamʿ*); nor can both disjuncts be false (*māniʿat al-khuluww*). Thus, in the example that al-Abharī cites in the section on disjunctive propositions, "numbers are either even or odd," only one of the two options can be true and neither of them can be false. A whole number must be either even or odd. It cannot be both and it cannot be neither. This means that the selection of one automatically eliminates the other. Syllogisms composed of strong disjunctive propositions in their premise are therefore valid regardless of whether the minor premise affirms or denies the disjunctive major premise.

Weak disjunctive syllogisms are more complicated. In a weak disjunctive proposition, the disjuncts can be both true or only one can be true. However, they cannot both be false. This means for a weak disjunctive syllogism to be valid, the minor premise can only deny one of the disjuncts to yield a necessary conclusion. An affirmation of a disjunct does not automatically mean that the other disjunct in the syllogism is false, since unlike a strong disjunctive syllogism, it is possible for both disjuncts of the major premise to be true. For example:

> Zayd wants to order either dinner or dessert.
>
> Zayd does not want to order dinner.
>
> Therefore, Zayd will order dessert.

A denial of one of the disjuncts above results in the other. However, an affirmation of one of the disjuncts does not mean the other one is false. If Zayd wants to order dinner, this does not mean that Zayd does not also want to order dessert (since the major premise here is a weak rather than strong disjunct). The mistake of assuming that an affirmation of a disjunct in a weak disjunctive syllogism results in the denial of the other is known as the **fallacy of affirming a weak disjunct.**

Translation

The Five Syllogistic Arts

[43] **Demonstration** (*burhān*) is a [type of] syllogism comprised of apodictic premises [from which] to derive certain conclusions.

[44] **Apodictic premises are divided into six categories**

[45] (1) **Axioms** (*awwaliyyāt*) like our statement, "one is half of two" or "the whole is greater than its parts."

[46] (2) **Observational Propositions** (*mushāhadāt*) like our statement, "the sun is bright," and "fire burns."

[47] (3) **Empirical Propositions** (*mujarrabāt*) like our statement, "drinks made of bindweed alleviate yellow bile."

[48] (4) **Intuitive Premises** (*ḥadsiyyāt*) like our statement, "the light of the moon is derived from the light of the sun."

[49] (5) **Recurrent mass transmitted** (*tawātur*) **reports** like our statement, "Muḥammad ﷺ proclaimed his prophecy," and "miracles were performed by his hand."

[50] (6) [**Innate Premises** (*fiṭriyyāt*)] are assertions that include syllogisms that must naturally accompany them because of a preconceived intermediate [principle] already present in the mind. For example, [we say] "four is an even [number]," because of the preconception that it [four] can be divided into two equal parts.

Explanatory Notes

The meaning of *burhān* (lit., "evidence" or "clear proof") varies based on its context. In the context of Qur'ānic studies, *al-Burhān* is another name for the Qur'ān. The Qur'ān refers to itself as *al-Burhān* (the decisive proof that elucidates right from wrong). In the context of Arabic logic, the word *burhān* represents the concept of *apodeixis*, as derived from Aristotle's *Posterior Analytics*. According to Aristotle, *apodeixis* refers to a demonstration that is a "deduction that produces knowledge."[23] Aristotle investigates how knowledge is derived to yield certainty using syllogisms. This means that not all syllogisms yield knowledge that is indisputably true if the premises are also indisputably true. As we see, some syllogisms evoke emotional responses that do not necessarily result in objectively true conclusions that result, by necessity, from unquestionably true premises. In Arabic this concept of the indisputable truth of a conclusion derived from true premises is described as *yaqīn* (Greek, *apodeixis*). An apodictic (*yaqīnī*) premise is one that is clearly established and does not require proof.

Propositions that are regarded as self-evident (*badīhiyyāt*) in their truth are divided into six categories. The first are axioms (*awwaliyyāt*). Axioms are known to be true without any intermediary to bring about a conclusion. They are regarded as self-evidently true and as a starting point on which further arguments can be built. Al-Abharī provides examples such as, "one is half of two" and "the whole is greater than its parts." In both cases, the conception of the subject and predicate are sufficient to establish the veracity of these propositional statements without the necessity of further syllogistic reasoning to demonstrate its truth. That is, the examples provided are true by their very definition.

If conceiving of the subject and the predicate in the mind is insufficient to establish the truth of a statement, then an intermediary is necessary to establish its truth. When the intermediary is an external

---

23 *Stanford Encyclopedia of Philosophy*: https://plato.stanford.edu/entries/aristotle-logic/#DemDemSci.

sense, the proposition is known as a sensible (*ḥissiyya*)[24] proposition and when the intermediary is an internal sense derived from introspective understanding, it is known as a reflective (*wijdāniyya*) proposition. When sensible and reflective propositions combine to form self-evident truths based on perception, they are called "observational propositions" (*mushāhadāt*). Al-Abharī provides examples such as, "the sun is bright" and "fire burns." In both cases, senses lead to introspective conclusions based on observations (one senses light with the eyes or heat with the limbs and concludes that the sun is bright and fire burns).

If the intermediary in deriving a judgment is present simultaneously with the conception of the subject and predicate, then it is known as an innate premise, or a "proposition whose logical conclusion is contained within them."[25] In Arabic logic, these types of innate premises are referred to as *fiṭriyyāt.* The text provides the following example: if we take it to be true that four is an even number, this leads to a simultaneously accepted truth that four can be divided into two even halves.

An "intuitive premise" (*ḥadsiyya*) is one in which a proposition does not have an obvious intermediary, yet thinking about the subject and predicate leads to an immediate intellectual connection and conclusion. That is, one naturally intuits a particular conclusion when the subject and predicate are presented. The text provides the example that the light of the moon is derived from the sun. While some may debate whether this knowledge is truly intuitive, at least without studying the natural sciences, regardless, when someone looks at the moon they generally make the connection that its light is reflected from the sun. Note that al-Abharī, who published this text almost a millennium ago, was familiar with the sophisticated tradition of astronomy in the

---

24 In this context, sensible (*ḥissiyya*) refers to what is perceptible by the senses.

25 Janis Esots, "al-Burhān," *Encyclopaedia Islamica*, online: https://referenceworks.brillonline.com/entries/encyclopaedia-islamica/burhan-COM_05000036?s.num=4&s.f.s2_parent=s.f.book.encyclopaedia-islamica&s.q=al-burhān.

Muslim world of his time—and in this tradition, it was commonly accepted that the moon's light comes from the sun.

"Unanimously circulated propositions" (*mutawātirāt*) are those in which a proposition is not intuitive or based on observation, but its truth is widespread and comes from multiple independent reports, such that the mind does not believe otherwise. Al-Abharī gives the following examples: "Muḥammad proclaimed his prophethood," and "miracles were performed at his hand." The concept of *tawātur* as recurrent mass transmitted reports means that multiple independent sources could not have colluded to cite this historical information, therefore, it must have actually happened.

Finally, "empirical propositions" (*tajribiyyāt*) are those in which a proposition is known to be true not because of a multiplicity of reports but because of a multiplicity of shared experiences. Al-Abharī gives the example of the remedial qualities of a particular flower, which when made into a drink, is useful for what he refers to as "yellow bile," a form of stomach affliction. The plant referred to in the example in the text is *saqmuniyya* (*convolvulus scammonia*), known in English as scammony, or more commonly, bindweed.

Finally, Muslim philosophers divided demonstrations into two categories: *burhān innī* and *burhān limmī.* These terms were originally derived from Aristotle's *Posterior Analytics*, in which demonstrations are categorized as *quia* or *propter quid.* Demonstrations which are *burhān innī* (Latin, *quia*) are based on premises from which the effect is known before the cause. These types of arguments are commonly structured to prove the existence of God. Thus, *burhān innī* (*quia*) demonstrations (in which the effects are the premises from which the cause is derived in the conclusion) include examples such as claiming that the sophistication of the world means that the world has a creator, or claiming that smoke means that there is a fire. *Innī* is derived from the word *inna*, a proposition used to emphasize the veracity of a statement, it means, "truly it is." *Innī* was originally translated from

Aristotle's term *quia*, which roughly means "that which is because," as it implies an effect, since an effect is "that which is because" of a cause.

Burhān innī are also known as *a posteriori* demonstrations, in which an effect is "posterior" or comes after a cause.

Burhān limmī are syllogisms in which the cause is known before the effect. The cause is mentioned in the premises and leads to the effect that is in the conclusion. These demonstrations are known from the Latin *propter quid* ("cause of something"), and are referred to as *a priori* demonstrations because the cause comes prior to the effect in the syllogism. *Limmī* is derived from the word *limā* ("why"). Thus, *burhān limmī* refers to a demonstration whose premises show why an effect is the case. That is, the cause ("the why") leads to the establishment of the effect as true. By contrast, a *burhān innī* demonstration starts with the effect as being an established truth and finds its cause in the conclusion.

Burhān Innī (*Quia*) Demonstration

Zaynab is a lawyer.

Anyone who is a lawyer must have gone to law school.

Therefore, Zaynab went to law school.

Burhān Limmī (*Propter Quid*) Demonstration

Anyone who wants to be a lawyer must go to law school.

Zaynab went to law school.

Therefore, Zaynab must be a lawyer.

In the first example, the effect (Zaynab is a lawyer) is stated as fact and is used to derive the cause that leads to it (that she must have gone to law school). In the second example, the causes are presented first and lead to the effect (that Zaynab is a lawyer) in the conclusion.

Effect → Cause = *Burhān Innī* (*Quia*)

Cause → Effect = *Burhān Limmī* (*Propter Quid*)

In addition to its relevance to questions of epistemology and the knowledge of God's existence in theological (*kalām*) literature, the way in which conclusions are derived also relates to fields such as jurisprudence (*fiqh*). *Fiqh* rulings that use demonstrative proofs based on *burhān limmī* are known as *qiyās al-ʿilla* and *fiqh* rulings derived from demonstrative proofs that are *burhān innī* are categorized as *qiyās al-dalāla*.[26]

26 Yusuf Şevki Yavuz, "Burhan," in *Islam Ansiklopedisi* (Istanbul: Türkiye Diyanet Vakfı, 1988), 6:429–430.

Translation

[51] **Dialectic** (*jadal*) is a syllogism composed of premises that are commonly accepted [as true].

[52] **Rhetoric** (*khaṭāba*) is a syllogism composed of premises accepted from a credible individual or [one whose opinions] are preferred.

[53] **Poetics** (*shiʿr*) are syllogisms composed of premises that bring joy to the heart or [cause it to] contract.

[54] **Sophistry** (*mughālaṭa*) are syllogisms composed of false premises that resemble the truth or commonly accepted [matters], or [they could be composed of] premises [based on] delusions [or superstitions] (*wahm*).

[55] The reliable [syllogism, in terms of accuracy and truth] is that of **demonstrative** [proofs] (*burhān*), nothing else. This is the end of the epistle on logic.

Explanatory Notes

Dialectic (*Jadal*)

Dialectic (*jadal*) is described as an argument based on premises that may not necessarily be true; however, they are commonly held to be true by the target audience. This idea of commonly held opinions is derived from Aristotle's concept of *endoxa* described in his *Topics* as ideas that are so well-established that they do not require examination. Commentaries on al-Abharī's *Isagoge* categorize these types of beliefs into the following.

[a] **Beliefs related to the greater good,** ***such as justice is good and oppression is wrong.***

[b] **Beliefs regarding compassion and kindness,** such as, "generosity toward the poor is praiseworthy," or "it is a duty to take care of the weak."

[c] **Beliefs related to safety, such as,** "protecting one's household is necessary," or "revealing one's nakedness in public is blameworthy."

[d] **Beliefs derived from customary practice,** such as, meat consumption is reprehensible for some while it is the norm for others.

This form of syllogism differs from syllogisms based on demonstrative proof (*burhān*) in key aspects, one of which is in the reliability of the truth on which the premises are based. In the absence of clearly established forms of demonstrative proofs, an individual engages in dialectic or debate with the intent of silencing or persuading his opponent by referencing commonly held opinions. This form of argumentation is weak because of the subjective nature of these opinions, because in order to be effective, they rely on assumptions that the audience must also share. The absence of an objectively verifiable statement in the form of demonstration makes these types of arguments vulnerable to deconstruction once the cognitive frameworks on which these arguments are made are shown to be faulty, or relative to one's perspective.

Rhetoric (*khaṭāba*)

Al-Abharī describes rhetoric as a form of persuasive speech in which the premises for one's argument are based on religious or dogmatic beliefs, such as the belief in miracles, the acceptance of scriptures as being derived from God's speech, or the miraculous feats of saints (*karāmāt al-awliyā'*). Alternatively, rhetoric (*khaṭāba*) can assume the truth of premises based on an appeal to commonly accepted authorities or experts (e.g., religious scholars, scientists, physicians, specialists in a particular field, or individuals regarded as saints with special gnostic capacities).[27]

The weakness of this approach is its reliance on the uniformity of the beliefs of the audience and those making the argument. The premises of the argument may not hold true to those who do not share common religious beliefs or who do not have confidence in the same expert authorities. The word for a religious sermon in Arabic is *khuṭba,* which shares the same root as *khaṭaba*. The type of speech in a *khuṭba* is one in which the speaker evokes shared religious beliefs with the audience; this enables him to persuade them or to move their hearts. Such a form of persuasive speech, however, may be less effective when addressed to those of other faiths.

Poetry (*Shiʿr*)

Poetry is composed of statements intended to spark the listeners' imagination by evoking emotional responses. Sometimes metaphors or similes are used, such as "roses are like rubies that emerge from the earth," or "her words pierced his heart like a dagger." Both phrases evoke an emotional response. Such creative language need not necessarily be false in their broader meaning. They may be false or true statements that are intended to rouse an audience's sentiment to make them partial to a particular opinion on an issue. This style can be presented in rhyme, prose, song, or speech.

Commentators on the *Isagoge* have raised the question as to whether imaginative words can be considered syllogisms. For instance, some may respond to this concern by saying that it is considered a form of persuasion and therefore, it is another way of making a case or arguing for a matter. Rather than appealing to the intellect, it appeals to the emotions because human emotions can persuade or dissuade people.[28]

27 Maḥmūd Ḥasan al-Maghnīsī, *Mughnī al-ṭullāb* (Damascus: Dār al-Bayrutī, 2009), 249–251.

28 al-Maghnīsī, *Mughnī al-ṭullāb*, 251.

For example, in the United States during the 1960s and 1970s, songs of protest were used by anti-war activists. Pep rallies for sports teams or battle music (e.g., the use of the *mehter* band by Ottomans during battles) are examples of this use of poetics to evoke specific emotions or opinions. National anthems are contemporary methods of strengthening a communal identity based on what are often carefully selected historical narratives, or myths, in the words of these songs. Other examples of the use of emotive language to elicit a sentimental response of anger, passion, or blind commitment can take the form of polemics. Polemical speeches may be political, religious, or other forms of divisive speech that create a strong supportive reaction in listeners.

More positive religiously-themed poetry takes the form of *mawlid*s (sung to evoke love for the Prophet Muḥammad during the celebration of his birth); these *mawlid*s engender a sense of communal devotion and individual belief in his prophecy. Similarly, among Shīʿī Muslims in particular, poetic recitations recalling the painful events of Karbala remind listeners of the tragedy of that day.

Sophistry (*Mughālaṭa*)

Sophistry is the use of arguments to influence opinion with premises based on logical fallacies that may appear to be true, or with deceptive statements. These types of false premises are not descriptions of senses or emotions, since describing matters that cannot be verified or denied does not fall under the types of sophistic statements mentioned.[29]

The term "sophistry" originates from Aristotle's *Sophistical Refutations*, in which he writes about false arguments that are commonly used to mislead listeners. During his time, individuals known as sophists used to perform these types of linguistic maneuverings for entertainment. Arabic logicians including al-Fārābī and Ibn Sīnā wrote commentaries on Aristotle's *Sophistical Refutations*; they translated this concept as *mughālaṭa* or *ṣafṣaṭa*. *Mughālaṭa* (from the root gh-l-ṭ)

---

29 Ibid., 252–253.

implies something that is incorrect, in this case incorrect arguments. *Ṣafṣaṭa* is a form of the word *ṣufiṣtā'iyya*; this is the term "sophistry" that appears in Aristotle's works and found its way into Islamic philosophy and logic.

The aim of such syllogisms is to manipulate language to misrepresent the truth, defeat an opponent in debate through word tricks, or appeal to commonly-held prejudices and desires to influence opinion rather than present rational arguments. Such speech is often used in political contexts to rally support or in polemics to promote an ideological position with aggressive appeals to emotion and reliance on logical fallacies.[30]

Ibn Sīnā wrote in his *Shifā'* that those who engage in sophistry (*mughālaṭa*) do so for three reasons: (1) Despite seeking the truth, they fall into logical fallacies because they have an insufficient understanding of sound arguments; (2) In order to defeat an opponent in a debate, they manipulate language or engage in deceptive games of logic; or (3) They want to appear knowledgeable about a matter and use demagoguery and logical fallacies to feign expertise.[31]

Samples of Logical Fallacies

1) **Equivocation** involves using a word in different ways throughout an argument. A word with multiple meanings, but which is consistently used in an argument with only one meaning, is said to be used univocally.

   Example: Only man [humans] is rational,

   and no woman is a man [male],

   therefore, no woman is rational.

   Here the word "man" may refer to humanity, or it may refer to a male human being. In this argument, in order to conclude that

30 Mahmut Kaya, "Mugalata," in *Islam Ansiklopedisi* (Istanbul: Türkiye Diyanet Vakfı, 1988), 30:372–373.

31 Ibid.

no woman is rational, there is a shift from the definition of "man" as a reference to humanity to "man" as a male.

2) **Straw Man arguments are those that** intentionally misrepresent the argument of one's opponent to make it seem ridiculous and/or to make it easier to rebut. Hence, one is creating a "straw man" that is easily brought down.

   Example: Society must support its needy population by providing free access to healthcare and education, which are not readily available because the system limits opportunities for some members.

   Straw man: You say that society should give free benefits to people without their working for it. Such a practice would encourage apathy and prevent people from striving to succeed.

3) ***Ad Hominem*** (Latin, "to the man") arguments are those in which one personally attacks the man or woman making the argument rather than engaging with the argument itself.

   Example: We are postponing our trip because of the impact of war on safety conditions in the countries we planned to visit.

   Ad hominem: You are postponing the trip because you prefer to stay at home.

   While it may be true, validly engaging an argument entails responding to the cause provided by the claimant, which in this case is safety on the trip. Attacking the opponent's motives does not disprove the argument and invalidates the response of the respondent.

4) **No True Scotsman** arguments are fallacies that occur when a claim is made about a mutually agreed on group of things or individuals. Rather than disputing the claim itself, the opponent engaging in this fallacy changes the terms of membership in this group.

   Example: Californians have difficulty adjusting to Chicago winters.

But, Nilufer is a Californian and she had no problem adjusting to Chicago winters.

No True Scotsman: Yes, but Nilufer is not a *real* Californian.

Here there is ambiguity over the definition of a Californian. This means that when contradictory evidence is presented, rather than readjusting her position, the claimant redefines who belongs in the group she is referring to.

5) **Not a Cause for a Cause** fallacy occurs when two events or things that may coincidentally overlap are assumed to have a causal relationship, when in fact their connection is only incidental.

   Example: According to Ibn Kathīr's *Bidāya wa-l-nihāya*, a solar eclipse occurred right after the death of the Prophet's son, Ibrāhīm.

   Not a Cause for a Cause: Some people said this is a sign from God for humans to mourn the Prophet's son. The Prophet responded to this by saying, the moon and the sun do not eclipse because of the life or death of any individual. That is, the relationship was deemed incidental and not "a cause for a cause."

   Another example: Everyone who passed the exam attended the gathering last night. Therefore, whoever attends this gathering before an exam will pass the exam.

   ʿAlī: This is not a cause for a cause. People who attended the gathering just happened to also study for and take the exam. They did not pass because of their presence at the meeting.

6) **Appeal to Fear** fallacy occurs when someone appeals to the fears of a group or an individual to persuade them rather using evidence.

   Example: Vote for my party's candidate for presidency. If the other candidate becomes president, she will raise taxes and repeal social security.

This argument uses fear to persuade a group into an action rather than presenting evidence that demonstrates that the candidate they support is the best person for the task.

7) **Guilt by Association** is an attempt to discredit an opponent's argument by indicating his association with a guilty party or detested group.

    Example: The study of logic is wrong because it entered Islamic thought through philosophers who were heretics.

    Such an argument is invalid because it assumes that the audience discredits philosophers for reasons of heresy and then it uses this bias to persuade the audience to be biased against a field of study associated with this group. The argument does not present any evidence pertaining to logic itself and does not offer reasons against its study.

8) **A False Dilemma** fallacy presents a limited set of options for the audience to select from, a set of options that is not in fact exhaustive of all of the possibilities. So the claimant creates a false dilemma by saying that one can only choose between a given set of options when in fact there are other options beyond this set.

    Example: ʿAlī must either attend college or be unemployed.

    The above argument does not assume any possibilities beyond these two options. ʿAlī could find gainful employment without going to college.

9) **An Appeal to the Bandwagon** argument presents the number of people who believe in something as evidence that it must be true.

    Example: If you want to have peace at home, make ginger tea for the family every Friday. Everyone in the neighborhood does this for the same purpose.

    The fact that "everyone" (or a number of people) does something does not make it true.

10) **An Appeal to Irrelevant Authority** fallacy occurs when a claimant uses a respected authority to support his argument even though the position of this authority figure is not relevant to the argument he is being used to support; this may be because he lacks the expertise in the matter he is being connected to or because his authority and/or popularity is unrelated to the topic under discussion.

Example: Imam ʿUmar, our beloved leader, said this flu medicine is the best in town.

Unless this spiritual leader also happens to be a medical practitioner with knowledge of medicines, using an audience's respect for him to persuade them about the quality of a cold medicine does not support the claimant's argument. The imam's religious authority is irrelevant in determining the best pharmaceutical products.

Glossary

affirmo (I affirm)
ʿaks al-mustawī (converse)
ʿāmm (general)
ʿaraḍ (accident); *ʿaraḍī* (accidental)
  ʿaraḍ ʿāmm (general accident)
  ʿaraḍ ʿāmm lāzim (inseparable general accident)
  ʿaraḍ ʿāmm mufāriq (separate general accident)
  ʿaraḍ khāṣṣ (specific accident)
  ʿaraḍ khass lāzim (specific attached/inseparable accident)
  ʿaraḍ khāṣṣ mufāriq (specific separable/detached accident)
  ʿaraḍ lāzim (attached accident)
  ʿaraḍ al-mufāriq (detached accident)
awwaliyyāt (axioms)

badīhiyyāt (self-evident)
al-baḥth wa-l-munāẓara (rational discourse and philosophy of debate)
burhān (demonstration; evidence; clear proof)
  burhān innī (Latin, *quia;* based on premises from which the effect is known before the cause; also known as *a posteriori* demonstrations)
  burhān limmī (Latin propter *quid;* a demonstration whose premises show why an effect is the case; also known as *a priori* demonstrations)

ḍarb, pl. *ḍurūb* (mood [of a syllogism]; Latin, *modus,* "way")
dhāt (essence; secondary substances); *dhātī* (essential)

exception (syllogisms of exception include terms such as "except" and "save")
exclusive syllogisms (compound syllogisms in which two parts of the syllogism are joined with terms such as "only" or "alone")

fallacy
  of affirming a weak disjunct (i.e., assuming that an affirmation of a disjunct in a weak disjunctive syllogism results in the denial

of the other)
of affirming the consequent (i.e., assuming the truth of the antecedent based on the truth of the consequent)
of denying the antecedent (i.e., assuming that a negation of the antecedent requires a negation of the consequent)
fourth term fallacy (i.e., a syllogism that is invalid because of an extra term)

faṣl (differentia)
fiʿl (act/action)
bi-l-fiʿl (in actuality)
fiqh (jurisprudence)
fiṭriyyāt (innate premises)

ḥadd (definition)
al-ḥadd al-akbar (major premise/term)
al-ḥadd al-aṣghar (minor premise/term)
al-ḥadd al-awsaṭ (middle term)
al-ḥadd al-nāqiṣ (incomplete definition)
ḥadd al-tāmm (complete definition)
ḥadsiyya (intuitive premise)
ḥaqīqa, pl. *ḥaqāʾiq* (true nature[s])
ḥaqīqa wāḥida (one true nature)
ḥaqīqī (real) [i.e., known in English logic as "strong" disjunctives]
ḥaqīqiyya (strong disjunctive proposition)
ḥaywān nāṭiq (rational animal)
ḥissiyya (sensible [proposition]; truth established through an intermediary that is an external sense)

iḍāfa (relationship; in logic, used to describe the relational connections between objects)
iltizām (association)
bi-l-iltizām (through association)
infiʿāl (affective)
iqtirānī (syllogisms of correlation)
istithnāʾī (selective [syllogism])
ittifāqiyya (lit., "concurrence"; in English logic, "contingent")

jadal (dialectic; a syllogism composed of premises that are commonly accepted as true)
jawhar (primary substance)

jins (genus)
juz'ī (particular)
juz'iyya musawwara (quantified particular proposition)

kalām (theology)
kammiyya (quantity)
kayfiyya (quality)
khabar (predicate [in the context of grammar])
khāṣṣ (specific)
khāṣṣa (property)
khaṭāba (rhetoric; a syllogism composed of premises accepted from a credible individual or [one whose opinions] are preferred)
khawāssihi al-lāzima (specific inseparable property)
kubrā (major [premise]; premise in a syllogism that includes the major term)
kullī (universal)
kulliyāt al-khams (five predicables)
kulliyya musawwara (quantified universal proposition)

lafẓ (utterance)
lām al-istighrāq (the indefinite article, i.e., "the")
lāzim (attached)
luzūmiyya (necessary; necessity of establishing a conclusion)

mabādi' al-taṣawwurāt (foundations of concepts)
mabādi' al-taṣdīqāt (foundations of assents)
māhiya (quiddity; 'what-ness')
maḥmūl (predicate, in the context of a categorical proposition)
maḥṣūratān (two quantified propositions)
makān (location)
māniʿat al-jamʿ (mutually exclusive)
māniʿat al-khuluww (cannot be collectively false)
maqāṣid al-taṣawwurāt (objectives of concepts)
maqāṣid al-taṣdīqāt (objectives of assents)
maʿqūlāt (intelligibles)
mawḍūʿ (subject)
modus ponens (method of affirming [Latin])
modus tollens (method of denying [Latin])
mu'allaf (compound)

mufrad (singular)
mughālaṭa (sophistry; syllogisms composed of false premises that resemble the truth or commonly accepted matters, or composed of premises based on delusions or superstitions (*wahm*))
muhmala (indefinite)
mujarrabāt (empirical propositions)
mūjiba (affirmative)
mulkiyya (possession)
munfaṣila (disjunctive)
muqaddam (antecedent)
muqaddima sharṭiyya (conditional premise that contains an if-statement)
mushāhadāt (observational propositions)
muta'akhkhirīn (post-classical [Ashʿarī theologians])
muṭābaqa (full correlation; words that convey meaning through exact definitions)
mutawātirāt (unanimously circulated propositions)

nāqiṣ (incomplete)
nawʿ (species)
nego (I deny)
nisba (relationship between assertions that establishes a conclusion by necessity, i.e., *luzūmiyya*)

qaḍiyya, pl. *qaḍāya* (proposition[s])
  qaḍiyya ḥamliyya (categorical proposition)
  qaḍiyya ittifāqiyya (contingent proposition)
  al-qaḍiyya al-makhṣūṣa (singular categorical propositions)
  qaḍiyya muhmala (indefinite propositions)
qawlun shāriḥ (expository statement)
qiyās (syllogism)
  qiyās al-dalāla (*fiqh* rulings derived from demonstrative proofs that are *burhān innī*)
  qiyās al-ʿilla (*fiqh* rulings that use demonstrative proofs based on *burhān limmī*)
  qiyās al-iqtirānī (syllogisms of correlation)
al-qiyās al-istithnā'ī (selective syllogism)
quwwa (capacity)
  bi-l-quwwa (in potentiality)
  quwwa wa-l-fiʿl (capacity and action)

rāfiʿa (negative selective syllogism)
al-rasm al-nāqiṣ (incomplete description)
al-rasm al-tāmm (complete description)
reductio ad absurdum (argument denying the consequent by means of demonstrating the absurdity of the antecedent)
reduplicative syllogism (distributes a predicate to a subject with specific conditions using phrases such as "as long as" and "as far as")

ṣafṣaṭa (sophistry; form of the word *ṣufiṣṭāʾiyya*)
sāliba (negative)
shakl (figure)
sharṭiyyatun munfaṣila (disjunctive conditional proposition)
sharṭiyyatun muṭṭaṣila (conjunctive conditional proposition)
shiʿr (poetics; syllogisms composed of statements intended to spark the listeners' imagination by evoking emotional responses)
al-ṣinaʿāt al-khams (five syllogistic arts)
ṣughrā (minor [premise])

tālī (consequent)
tanāquḍ (opposition)
tasalsul (infinite regress)
taṣawwurāt (concepts)
taṣdīqāt (assents)
tawātur (recurrent mass transmitted [reports])

waḍʿ (position in the context of ten categories)
wahm (delusions, superstitions)
wijdāniyya (reflective [proposition]; truth established through an intermediary that is an internal sense derived from introspective understanding)
wujūd (existence)

yaqīn (Greek, *apodeixis;* concept of the indisputable truth of a conclusion derived from true premises)

zamān (time)

Bibliography

Adamson, Peter. *Philosophy in the Islamic World: A History of Philosophy Without Any Gaps*. Oxford: Oxford University Press, 2016.

Adamson, Peter and Alexander Key. "Philosophy of Language in the Medieval Arabic Tradition." In *Linguistic Meaning: New Essays in the History of the Philosophy of Language*, edited by Margaret Cameron and Robert J. Stainton, 74–99. Oxford: Oxford University Press, 2015.

Alp, Talha. *Mantık: Isagoci Tercümesi ve Mantık Terimleri Sözlüğü*. Istanbul: Yasin Yayınevi, 2009.

Anawati, G. C. "Abharī, Aṯīr-al-dīn." In *Encyclopædia Iranica*, I/2: 216–217. Online: https://referenceworks.brillonline.com/entries/encyclopaedia-iranica-online/abhari-atir-al-din-COM_4455?s.num=2&s.f.s2_parent=s.f.book.encyclopaedia-iranica-online&s.q=Abharī.

al-Anṣārī, Zakariyyā. *al-Maṭlaʿ sharḥ Īsāghūjī.* Kuwait: Dār al-Ḍiyāʾ, 2017.

Barnes, Jonathan. *Porphyry: Introduction*. Oxford: Oxford University Press, 2003.

Bingöl, Abdulkuddüs. "Ebheri, Esirüddin." In *Islam Ansiklopedisi*, 10:75–76. Istanbul: Türkiye Diyanet Vakfı, 1988.

Bingöl, Abdulkuddüs. "Īsāgūcī." In *Islam Ansiklopedisi*, 22:488–489. Istanbul: Türkiye Diyanet Vakfı, 1988.

Calverley, Edwin. "al-Abharī's *Īsāghūjī fī 'l-Manṭiq*," 73–85. In *The Macdonald Presentation Volume*. London: Oxford University Press, 1933.

Damer, T. Edward. *Attacking Faulty Reasoning.* Belmont: Wadsworth Cengage Learning, 2009.

Emiroğlu, Ibrahim. "Mantık." In *Islam Ansiklopedisi*, 28:18–28. Istanbul: Türkiye Diyanet Vakfı, 1988.

Griffel, Frank. *The Formation of Post-Classical Philosophy in Islam*. Oxford: Oxford University Press, 2021.

Gyekye, Kwame. "The Term Istithnā' in Arabic Logic." *Journal of the American Oriental Society* 92, no. 1 (Jan.–Mar. 1972): 88–92.

Inati, Shams. "Ibn Sina on Single Expressions." In *Islamic Theology and Philosophy: Studies in Honor of George Hourani*, edited by Michael E. Marmura, 148–159. Albany: State University of New York Press, 1984.

Kaya, Mahmut. "Mugalata." In *Islam Ansiklopedisi*, 30:372–373. Istanbul: Türkiye Diyanet Vakfı, 1988.

Key, Alexander. *Language Between God and the Poets*. Berkeley: University of California Press, 2018.

Kreeft, Peter. *Socratic Logic: A Logic Text Using Socratic Method, Platonic Questions, and Aristotelean Principles*. South Bend, IN: St. Augustine's Press, 2004.

al-Maghnīsī, Maḥmūd Ḥasan. *Mughnī al-ṭullāb: Sharḥ matn Īsāghūjī.* Damascus: Dār al-Bayrutī, 2009.

Özpilavcı, Ferruh. *Ebheri Isaguci ve Şerhi*. Istanbul: Litera Yayıncılık, 2020.

Stanford Encyclopedia of Philosophy. Edited by Edward N. Zalta. Stanford, CA: Metaphysics Research Lab. Online: https://plato.stanford.edu/.

Sullivan, Scott. *An Introduction to Traditional Logic: Classical Reasoning for Contemporary Minds.* North Charleston, SC: Booksurge Publishing, 2006.

Yavuz, Yusuf Şevki. "Burhan." In *Islam Ansiklopedisi*, 6:429–430. Istanbul: Türkiye Diyanet Vakfı, 1988.

www.ingramcontent.com/pod-product-compliance
Lightning Source LLC
LaVergne TN
LVHW051001080826
845145LV00009B/2393

9780578331270